The
Devotional
Qur'an

The Devotional Qur'an

Beloved Surahs and Verses

SELECTED AND TRANSLATED BY

SHAWKAT M. TOORAWA

Yale UNIVERSITY PRESS/NEW HAVEN & LONDON

Published with assistance from the foundation established in memory of
James Wesley Cooper of the Class of 1865, Yale College.

Yale University Press books may be purchased in quantity for
educational, business, or promotional use. For information, please e-mail
sales.press@yale.edu (U.S. office) or sales@yaleup.co.uk (U.K. office).

Designed by Mary Valencia.
Set in Electra type by Integrated Publishing Solutions.
Printed in the United States of America.

Library of Congress Control Number: 2023944294
ISBN 978-0-300-27194-2 (hardcover : alk. paper)

A catalogue record for this book is available from the
British Library.

This paper meets the requirements of ANSI/NISO Z39.48-
1992 (Permanence of Paper).

10 9 8 7 6 5 4 3 2 1

pou isaal-e sawaab
nou zanfan zot granparan,
fareenani,
ek dada baba

a 'ûdhu billâhi min ash-shaytânir rajîm
bismillâhir rahmânir rahîm

Alif Lâm Mîm

This is Scripture, doubtless and unwavering
Guidance for the pious and the reverent
who believe in the Unseen
whose Prayer is constant
and who are bountiful with the livelihood We provide

Who believe in what We reveal to you
in what we revealed to those who precede you
and who are confident in the life to come!

Rightly guided by their Lord
they will be victorious
they will be triumphant!

(Baqarah 2:1–5)

CONTENTS

ACCORDING TO MUSLIM BELIEF, in the year 610 the Arch-
angel Gabriel appeared to Muhammad—who was on one of
his frequent retreats to a cave outside Mecca for spiritual con-
templation—and uttered the following words, in Arabic:

> Proclaim in the name of your Lord
> who created Humankind
> from a simple clot—
>
> Proclaim: Your Lord is Generous—
> through the pen He taught
> Human beings what they did not know.

('Alaq 96:1–5)

Shaken by this encounter, Muhammad was convinced he was
losing his mind. He ran home to his wife Khadîjah for conso-
lation. Together with a pious Christian relative, she reassured
Muhammad that his vision was real, and that the being was
indeed Gabriel, bringing God's Word to him. He had become,
in other words, a chosen prophet. Over the course of the next
twenty-three years, Gabriel continued to appear periodically to
Muhammad and to bring revelation from God. Muhammad's
followers, who came to be known as Muslims—meaning those
who submit (islâm) to God's will—memorized those revela-
tions in turn, wrote them down, and disseminated them. In the
nearly millennium and a half since, those revelations have

constituted Islam's sacred scripture, the Qur'an, literally The Recitation.[1] For Muslims, reading or reciting the Arabic Qur'an is an act of devotion. Pious Muslims continue to read and recite the Qur'an throughout their lives; in many communities, the first time a Muslim completes a full reading (*khatm*) is a cause of public celebration.

Today, Muslims number just under two billion, or a quarter of the world's population. As in other religions and belief systems, they run the gamut: there are devout Muslims, cultural Muslims, conservative Muslims, progressive Muslims, Muslims from birth, Muslims who have converted, Muslims who adhere to a denomination, Muslims who have no affiliation, and many other kinds besides. All have heard the rhythms of the Qur'an permeating their soundscape, often in childhood, at home, at school, or at the mosque. Observant Muslims are bound together by three beliefs: belief in the prophethood of Muhammad; belief in the divine origin and nature of the Arabic Qur'an—the teachings, injunctions, and prohibitions of which are held to be binding; and belief in the existence of one true God, who is characterized as follows in Surah Hashr (The Mustering, 59):

He is God
There is no god but He

Sovereign
Holy
Serene

Protecting
and True

Exalted
Commanding
Magnificent

Exalted far above
what they can portray

(Hashr 59:22–23)

To testify that there is no deity except the one true God (Allah) and that Muhammad is his prophet (*lâ ilâha ill allâh, muhammadun rasûl allâh*) is the fundamental creed or doctrinal belief of Islam, a formulation known as the *shahâdah*, a testimony that every Muslim must utter at least once in their lifetime, and which one often finds adorning the entryways to homes. What this testimony entails is conveyed in the Detailed Articles of Belief (*îmân mufassal*): "I believe in God, in His angels, in His scriptures, in His prophets, in the Last Day, in destiny, both good and bad, and in resurrection after death."[2] This underscores the fact that Islam sees itself as part of a continuous process of revelation of God's will to humanity, through angels, scriptures, and prophets such as Adam, Idrîs, Noah, David, Shu'ayb, John the Baptist, and Jesus, to name only a few of the hundred and twenty-four thousand believed to have been sent by God to all of humankind. It is therefore no surprise that the Qur'an accepts, co-opts, and, in its own view, corrects what was revealed in earlier monotheistic scriptures. In doing so, it emphasizes that its message is no different from the revelation God had vouchsafed to innumerable prophets, including Abraham and Moses. Indeed, it is a continuation of that revelation:

> Those who purify themselves and prosper
>   shall invoke their Lord and engage in Prayer.
>
> Still, it's life in this world you prefer.
>   But the Hereafter is infinitely better!
>
> This was made clear in what We already sent you—
>   Abraham's Scrolls, and Moses' Scripture.
>
> (A'lâ 87:17–19)

From the start, then, Muhammad preached Islam as part of God's grace to all humanity.[3]

My first engagement with the Qur'an in Arabic was as a very young child in Paris, hearing and then memorizing short surahs and other devotional passages my parents would recite to me. That was followed by early instruction from a remarkable Senegalese tutor, Shaykh Abdullah Diop. When we moved to Singapore, my parents hoped the teacher they engaged there, the learned Tamil scholar Maulvi M. H. Babu Sahib, would make a decent reciter of Qur'an out of me. I never became any good at measured recitation, but from Maulvi Babu Sahib

I did learn a great deal of what I know about Islamic law, Islamic tradition, and Muslim observance.

My first engagement with the Qur'an in English was reading the translation by Abdullah Yusuf Ali. We had a few other translations in our home, but it was Yusuf Ali's that captivated me. Part of the appeal came from the headnotes he placed before each surah, together with summaries he crafted in blank verse, and part from the many thousands of extensive scholarly and personal footnotes that drew liberally from the Arabic commentary tradition, from other scriptures, and from English literature.[4] I was also drawn by the language of the translation, a neo-Victorian English that sounded to me very much the way I, still only a boy, thought God would sound — *should* sound — in English:

> It is God Who has
> Made the Night for you,
> That ye may rest therein,
> And the Day, as that
> Which helps (you) to see.
> Verily God is Full of
> Grace and Bounty to men:
> Yet most men give
> No thanks.[5]

A few years later, when I began to think seriously about university, I had no idea what to study or what career to pursue. I decided I should learn a new language, one that would allow me to read its literature in the original. I settled on Arabic. Like the vast majority of Muslims—eighty percent of the world's Muslims are not Arab and have no mastery of Arabic—I knew how to read and intone the Arabic of the Qur'an but could not understand what I was reading. Muslims believe not only in the sacrosanct nature of God's original revelation in Arabic and the truth of its message, but equally in the beauty and power of its sounds *as Arabic*, and in the value and potential of the original in the liturgy and daily devotions; this is why so many Muslims continue to cherish recitation of a text they do not understand.

My only study of the Qur'an as an undergraduate and graduate student was one seminar with the great Jesuit Qur'an scholar Gerhard Böwering. This is not to say that the Qur'an did not come up in the course of my studies—its rhythms, cadences, influences, and expressions permeate the Arabic literary tradition, much in the same way that the King James Bible does the English one: it simply was not a text I studied directly.

This would change on account of three events.

The first took place in Ramadan of 1989, on a family trip to Medina. During the predawn ritual prayer at the Prophet's Mosque, congregants, myself included, were transported by the beautiful surah the imam chose to recite. I wasn't completely certain which surah it was, so I went to a bookshop, sought out a Qur'an concordance, and looked up a memorable word from the surah: *zanjabîl*, ginger. The imam had recited

Surah Insân (Humankind, 76), which the Prophet Muham-
mad recommended be recited in the morning prayer. When I
looked closely at the surah on the page, I was struck again by
the large number of unusual rhyme words, such as *zamharîr*,
biting cold, and *qawârîr*, crystal, and astonished when I real-
ized that in none of the translations that I consulted had the
translators paid attention to internal rhythm or rhyme.[6] When
I returned to Cairo, where I was spending the year, I tried my
hand at translating the surah: I wanted to see if it was possible
to produce a rhyming translation. It was.

The second formative event was in September 1996. I was
living in Mauritius and my uncle Firoz Toorawa, who had been
in Medina in 1989 and who remembered my unhappiness with
English translations then available, asked me to produce a
translation of Surah Yâ Sîn (36): it is virtuous and a pious act to
publish and distribute surahs as self-standing booklets, often
upon the death of a loved one, the idea being that when the
recipient reads from the collection, divine reward will accrue
to the deceased. I agreed, and as with my earlier attempt to
translate Surah Insân, I strove to find appropriate rhyme sounds
in English.

The third event was in November 2005, at the biennial
Qur'an Conference hosted by the Centre for Islamic Studies
at the University of London. After I had presented my paper,
Professor Muhammad Abdel Haleem—director of the Cen-
tre, a leading Qur'an scholar, a *hâfiz* (someone who has the
whole Qur'an memorized), and editor of the *Journal of Qur'anic*

Studies—took me aside and said, "I know you work on Arabic literature, medieval Baghdad, and so on. Good. Work on the Qur'an." Emboldened by Professor Abdel Haleem's encouragement, I began engaging more deeply with the sacred text and translating more surahs. The emotional power and musical qualities of the Qur'an have moved listeners and readers for nearly fifteen hundred years. When I translated, therefore, I felt strongly the need to mirror the pervasive and cadenced rhythmic prose (termed *saj '*) that characterizes the Qur'anic text. As I did so, the view often expressed to me was that it is too difficult, perhaps even impossible, to translate the Qur'an's "semantic multidimensionality" and still retain the meaning. But to ignore the Qur'an's rhythms and rhymes is to imply that these are unimportant components of the Qur'anic text, something that would never be said of the original.[7] I wanted colleagues to be able to give their students translations that were as attentive as possible to the Qur'an's soundscape.[8]

When I made the decision to bring my translations together into a book, two things became clear to me about my efforts up to that point, however: I had hewed too closely to the original Arabic syntax, and the rhymes I'd chosen were overly stiff and conspicuous. The translations needed the eye and ear of a poet. I mustered up the courage to approach Peter Cole, distinguished poet and translator, and dear friend. Under his guidance, I began to improve what I had translated.

In the translations that follow, I try to accomplish several things. First, I want to show that, difficult as it is to translate the Qur'an while being attentive to rhyme, it is certainly not impossible. Second, I want to demonstrate that meaning inheres in the deployment of sounds in the Qur'an. Third, I want to convince readers and listeners that the sonorous qualities of Qur'anic Arabic can be conveyed to a non-Arabic readership and listenership. And fourth, I want to make clear that inattention to the original's rhetorical and literary character comes at a great cost, one only underscored by the fact that many millions of readers interact with the Qur'an in translation.[9]

I have tried also to be attentive to the different types of speech in the Qur'an, the diversity of which is flattened by almost all translators, typically into continuous prose on the English page. The handful of exceptions are Arberry, Cleary, Khalidi, Sells, and Yusuf Ali.[10] Khalidi, for instance, writes:

> The "register" of the Qur'an constantly shifts, from narrative to exhortation, from homily to hymn of praise, from strict law to tender sermon, from fear and trembling to invitations to reflection. These, I decided, *had* to look different, hence the horizontal and vertical disposition of the translation.[11]

He is, in a way, following Arberry, who also strategically positions the verses and words on the page. Eschewing rhyme, for instance, he notes:

> I have preferred to indicate these terminations and connections by rounding off each succession of rhythms with a much shorter

line . . . I have called attention to . . . changes in mood and
tempo by making corresponding variations in my own rhythmi-
cal patterns.[12]

I avail myself of these techniques and others when they can
contribute to the force of the translation and to the visuality of
the reading experience. I too center Surah Rahmân (The Ever
Compassionate, 55) on the page, for example, as well as Surah
Insân (Humankind, 76). I break the short, staccato-like surahs
into stanzas; I use uppercase and italics liberally to mirror em-
phasis and rhetorical features in the Arabic; and I nest stories
and parables to signal the start of discrete narratives. Here is an
example from Surah Kahf (The Cave, 18):

We recount their Story accurately—

> The story of youths who believed in their Lord, youths rewarded
> with Guidance for their Piety ◆ We bolstered them when they
> stood firm saying, *"Our Lord is Lord of Heaven and Earth—we
> shall never call on any other deity! That would be calumny!"* ◆
> *"Our people worship idols instead! Can they produce a basis for
> this, a clear authority! Can anyone be more corrupt than fabrica-
> tors, opposing God with their iniquity?"* ◆ and when they advised
> one another: *"And when you have forsworn them and what they
> worship besides God, let us retreat to a Cave where God shall
> shower you with His Clemency—In this time of need shall He
> provide comfort"* ◆

(Kahf 18:13–16)

A distinctive challenge facing translators of the Qur'an is the belief held by many Muslims that the Arabic of the Qur'an, as a manifestation and translation of God's Word and Will into human language, is ultimately untranslatable. Like so many other scriptures, the Qur'an has nevertheless been translated into almost every language of the world, including about a hundred or so full translations into English to date. Indeed, hundreds of millions of Muslims and non-Muslims have turned and continue to turn to such translations to uncover, discover, and even refute its message. As a result, many translators of the Qur'an opt to render the Arabic as literally as possible. To do so, however, neglects fifteen centuries of Qur'an scholarship by Muslims that insists that the Qur'an makes meaning on multiple levels — indeed, that that is one of its defining features and an aspect of its divine origin and miraculous nature (*i'jâz*). For instance, in his commentary on the expression *laylat al-qadr*, "Night of Qadr" (from Surah Qadr [Awe, 97]), the twelfth-century traditionalist religious scholar Ibn al-Jawzî explains:

> There are five opinions regarding why *laylat al-qadr* is so named.

> — The first is that *qadr* means "glory," as in the expression "he is possessed of glory (*qadr*)." This is al-Zuhrî's view and is borne out by its use in God's words, "They do not adequately reckon God's glory (*qadr*)" [An'âm 6:91].

—The second is that it denotes constraint; hence it is a night on which the earth is constrained by the angels descending upon it. This is al-Khalîl's view and is borne out by its use in God's words, "Whosoever's livelihood is constrained (*qudira*)" [Talâq 65:7].

—The third is that *qadr* means "decree," inasmuch as things are decreed (*tuqaddaru*) on that night. This is Ibn Qutaybah's view.

—The fourth is by virtue of the fact that all those without standing (*qadar*), by dint of their observance of the night, thereby acquire standing. This is Abû Bakr al-Warrâq's view.

—The fifth is because an exalted (*qadar*) Book descended that night, exalted Mercy descended that night, and exalted angels too. This is the view of our teacher 'Alî ibn 'Abdallâh.[13]

This gloss is one example among thousands that show clearly that the Muslim commentarial tradition embraces the multiplicity of Qur'anic meanings and interpretations. And, in fact, this is reflected in multiple translations: in four recent ones by Muslims, the expression *laylat al-qadr* is rendered four different ways: Night of Power, Night of Glory, Night of Decree, and Night of Destiny.[14] My own translation of Surah Qadr reads:

> We sent it down on the Night of Awe—
> What, you ask, is the Night of Awe?
>
> The Night of Awe is better by far
> than a thousand months or more

> A Night when angels and Spirit descend
> > charged by their Lord
>
> A Night of peace—
> > Peace, till the break of dawn

(Qadr, 97)

Being faithful to the Qur'anic text in English translation does not, ultimately, mean finding an exact or literal English equivalent—more often than not, there is no such thing, either because no truly literal translation exists or, as with the example presented above, because there is no consensus as to what the literal meaning of a given word is, or because the consensus is that there is an intended plurality of meanings.

Knowledge about the early history of the Qur'an comes from three main sources: from the Qur'an itself—its contents and also the material history of early Qur'anic fragments, such as the dating of very early manuscripts; from the hadith corpus— the faithful recollection of statements and deeds of the Prophet Muhammad, not unlike the canonical gospels in the Christian tradition; and from the biographies (*sîrah*) of Muhammad— reverent collections recounting events both chronologically and topically.[15] According to the *sîrah*, Muhammad initially preached his message to those close to him, a small group of family members and confidants. These women and men around Muhammad, called *sahâbâ*, Companions, scrupulously memorized the revelations he repeated to them and also his words of advice and exhortation. By following the prescriptions of the Qur'an and by heeding the instruction of Muhammad and emulating his deeds as recorded in hadiths, the early Muslims, and Muslims after them, honor the Qur'anic injunction to obey God and His prophet (Ahzâb 33:71).

The parts of the Qur'an widely held to contain the earliest revelations date to the time when Muhammad and his small group of followers were living in Mecca; they resembled the oracular pronouncements of Arabian soothsayers, whose terse statements were also in rhyming prose (*saj'*). But unlike the latter's mundane predictions and their attachment to a plurality of local gods, the message Muhammad brought focused on belief in one true, just, and merciful God, on the end-time and the Day of Judgment, on acts of charity, and on right action, as in the following verse:

> To be constant in Prayer and give freely in charity.
> This is the true declaration of devotion.

> (Bayyinah 98:5)

Persecution by the Meccans who continued to believe in their local gods led Muhammad to dispatch a small group of his most vulnerable followers to Abyssinia, where he knew they would be welcomed by its Christian king. Several years later, Muhammad was approached by citizens of the northern Arabian oasis town of Yathrib to act as a mediator in an ongoing local feud. Muhammad and his Meccan followers, less than a hundred in all, emigrated there in the year 622 (called the *hijrah*). The community now had a permanent settlement where they were all welcome. In time, Muhammad became the leader of the city, which became known as Medina (from *Madînat al-Nabî*, City of the Prophet), and the populace embraced Islam. From the arrival of the Muslims in Medina until Muhammad's death ten years later in 632, the Qur'anic revelations reflected more and more the Prophet's role as leader of a community proper (*ummah*). To this period are dated the Qur'an's longer surahs, which often include a combination of parables, narratives of earlier communities, admonition, legislative material, and descriptions of the afterlife, both the Garden and the Fire.[16]

Western scholars of the Qur'an have long been attracted to those parts of the Qur'an that help account for the theologies that developed from it, that help explain the book's early textual history, and that allow for a comparison with other scriptural traditions, including the Hebrew Bible and the Gospels. And Western translators, from the mid-seventeenth century up until the mid-twentieth century, were by and large hostile to Islam, using the vehicle of translation to expose what they believed was a fraudulent religion and what they regarded as an incoherent text.[17] More recent translators, for their part — especially Muslims, who represent the vast majority of translators in the past hundred years — have been attracted to the prospect of producing a new translation that will reveal why Muslims revere the Qur'an and live by it, why it is "the divine arbiter of Muslim life."[18] That said, when one reads the entire Qur'an in translation, it is all but impossible to discern which parts are important in the lives of practicing Muslims. The story of Mary and Jesus, for example, plays a central role in theology and interreligious debate but Surah Maryam (Mary, 19) is not often recited in devotional or liturgical contexts; most Muslims therefore know it less well than they do, say, Surah Yâ Sîn (36), one longer surah that is regularly read and recited.

Devotional practices vary greatly over time, across regions, and among communities and denominations, but all are rooted in the practice of earlier figures, mainly the Prophet, but also his closest Companions, the Shiite Imams, saintly figures, learned scholars, Sufi masters, one's local imam or religious teacher, or one's parents and forbears. Even seemingly personal practices are learned from family members and teachers. There are accordingly portions of the Qur'an that hold a special place in the hearts of Muslims, surahs and passages that they commit to memory, read in groups, or read silently as acts of devotion. Indeed, the different communal, denominational, doctrinal, and regional traditions share a core of surahs and passages.[19]

In choosing which specific surahs and passages to translate, I decided to focus on ones that Muslims turn to in their devotions—notably in daily ritual prayers (*salât*), in supplications (*du ʿâ*), and in pious remembrance (*dhikr*).[20] And in organizing the collection, I have used two broad overlapping principles:

sequencing the surahs and passages in roughly the order in which Muslims encounter and memorize them, and organizing them according to devotional use. My selection is by no means comprehensive and is inevitably inflected by my own experiences as a South Asian Sunni Muslim.[21] I have, however, endeavored to include surahs and passages which Muslims will immediately recognize as central to practice and to devotion and invoked in the context of prayer, supplication, and remembrance.[22] In short, I have given pride of place to those surahs and passages that matter deeply to Muslims — rendered in a way that is attentive to the Qur'an's sounds and rhythms — and sequenced them as follows:

> The Fâtihah
> The short surahs (the last twenty-two)
> Âyat al-Kursî
> Surah Yâ Sîn
> Surahs recited daily or weekly (*Naba'*, *Wâqi'ah, Mulk, Rahmân, Insân*)
> Friday verses and surahs (six passages; *A'lâ, Ghâshiyah, Kahf*)
> Verses glorifying God (thirteen passages)
> Supplication verses (ten passages)

In these translations, then, I've sought to do two things: to provide a representative example of the Qur'an as many Muslims know it in a devotional context, and to account for the presence of rhythm and sound within that experience. Each section is preceded by a headnote describing the place and role of the verse, passage, or surah in Muslim devotional practice. I also provide brief endnotes to explain specific translation choices or context; a glossary of terms; an appendix giving a selection of illustrative popular *wazîfah*s, or recitation practices; and an index listing surahs and passages translated here and the corresponding page numbers.

In Arabic, the Qur'an is beautiful, sonorous, supple, moving, persuasive, demiurgic. It is my hope that some glimmers of this emerge in the efforts below.[23]

Notes

1. Fine introductions to the Qur'an are Ingrid Mattson, *The Story of the Qur'an: Its History and Place in Muslim Life*, 2nd ed. (Chichester, West Sussex: Wiley-Blackwell, 2013), and Anna M. Gade, *The Qur'an: An Introduction* (Oxford: Oneworld, 2016).

2. The first half of the creed mirrors a passage in Baqarah 2:285.

3. Accessible introductions to Islam include Rageh Omaar et al., *The Islam Book: Big Ideas Simply Explained* (London: Dorling Kindersley, 2020); the essays in Roger Allen and Shawkat M. Toorawa, eds., *Islam: A Short Guide to the Faith* (Grand Rapids, MI: William B. Eerdmans, 2011); and Kecia Ali and Oliver Leaman, *Islam: The Key Concepts* (London: Routledge, 2008).

4. Yusuf Ali cites from Shakespeare's Sonnet 94, for instance, when commenting on Baqarah 2:30. Abdullah Yusuf Ali, trans., *The Holy Qur-an: Text, Translation, and Commentary*, 2 vols. (New York: Hafner, 1938), 1:24n47.

5. Yusuf Ali, *The Holy Qur-an*, 2:1279. The verse is Mu'min 40:61.

6. The translations of Cleary (1993), Sells (1999), and Khalidi (2008) had not yet appeared (see note 10 below). Arberry does, it is true, privilege "rhetorical and rhythmical patterns which are the glory and the sublimity of the Koran" (Preface to A. J. Arberry, trans., *The Koran Interpreted*

[London: George Allen and Unwin, 1955], 25). But his translation of Surah Insân sounded flat (and dated) to me; this is verse 6: "a fountain whereat drink the servants of God,/making it to gush forth plenteously" (315).

7. "Semantic multidimensionality" is Michael Sells's apt characterization in "Sound, Spirit and Gender in *Sūrat al-Qadr*," *Journal of the American Oriental Society* 111, no. 2 (1991): 259.

8. These translations have appeared in the *Journal of Qur'anic Studies*, volumes 4 (2002), 8 (2006), 9 (2007), 13 (2011), 15 (2013), 17 (2015), 23 (2021), and 24 (2022).

9. This is poet and translator Alicia Stallings on not translating rhyme: "Translators who translate poems that rhyme into poems that don't rhyme solely because they claim that keeping the rhyme is impossible without doing violence to the poem have done violence to the poem." A. E. Stallings, "Presto Manifesto!" *Poetry* 193, no. 5 (2009): 451.

10. Arberry, *The Koran Interpreted*; Thomas Cleary, trans., *The Essential Koran: The Heart of Islam. An Introductory Selection of Readings from the Qur'an* (San Francisco: HarperSanFrancisco, 1993); Tarif Khalidi, trans., *The Qur'an: A New Translation* (London: Penguin, 2008); Michael Sells, *Approaching the Qur'an: The Early Revelations*, 2nd ed. (Ashland, VT: White Cloud, 2007); Yusuf Ali, *The Holy Qur-an*.

11. Khalidi, *The Qur'an: A New Translation*, xx–xxi.

12. Arberry, *The Koran Interpreted*, 25–26.

13. Ibn al-Jawzî, *Zâd al-masîr fî 'ilm al-tafsîr*, 8 vols. (Beirut: Dâr al-Kutub al-'Ilmiyyah, 1994), 8:182.

14. These are the renderings of Khalidi, Abdel Haleem, Saheeh International [Emily Assami, Mary Kennedy, Amatullah Bantley], trans. *The Qur'an* (Jeddah: Abul-Qasim, 1997), and Waheeduddin Khan and Farida Khanam, trans. *The Quran* (Delhi: Goodword, 2014).

15. An influential *sîrah* is Ibn Ishâq, *The Life of Muhammad: A Translation of Ibn Ishâq's Sîrat Rasûl Allâh*, trans. Alfred Guillaume (Karachi: Oxford University Press, 1955).

16. According to the celebrated tenth-century commentator al-Tabarî, the Qur'an consists of seven types of speech: "command, prohibition,

promise, threat, argument, narrative, and similitude." See Tabarî, *Selections from "The Comprehensive Exposition of the Interpretation of the Verses of the Qur'ân*," 2 vols., trans. Scott C. Lucas (Cambridge: The Royal Aal Al-Bayt Institute and The Islamic Texts Society, 2017), 1:37.

17. For a survey of this antagonism, see Arberry, Preface to *The Koran Interpreted*, 7–24; Franz Volcker Greifenhagen, "*Traduttore, Traditore*: An Analysis of the English Translations of the Qur'an," *Islam and Muslim-Christian Relations* 3, no. 2 (1992): 274–91; and Bruce B. Lawrence, *The Koran in English: A Biography* (Princeton, NJ: Princeton University Press, 2017), 29–49.

18. Khalidi, *The Qur'an: A New Translation*, ix.

19. See the Appendix of Wazîfahs for a selection of *wazîfahs*, or recommended recitation practices. The virtues of specific surahs and passages are called the *fadâ'il al-Qur'ân* ("Merits/Virtues/Qualities of the Qur'an"). The Prophet Muhammad extolled the virtues of the Qur'an in general and also of specific surahs and passages in particular: there is, therefore, often a section in hadith collections devoted to these. The *fadâ'il al-Qur'ân* also constitutes an early genre, whereby authors compiled books enumerating the virtues of the Qur'an, and also often the etiquette associated with reading and reciting it. For hadiths about the merits of the surahs I include here, see, e.g., *Sahîh al-Bukhârî*, the canonical ninth-century hadith collection of al-Bukhârî, part 66 of which is devoted to *fadâ'il*: see https://sunnah.com/bukhari/66; Tabarî, *Selections*, 23–29; and Ibn al-Jazarî, *Al Hisn Al Haseen* (Karachi: Darul Ishaat, 2008), 408–38.

20. On the types of worship and prayer in Islam, see Shawkat M. Toorawa, "Prayer," in *Key Themes for the Study of Islam*, ed. Jamal J. Elias (Oxford: Oneworld, 2010), 263–81. See also Constance Padwick, *Muslim Devotions: A Study of Prayer-Manuals in Common Use* (Oxford: Oneworld, 1996 [1961]), and Marion Katz, *Prayer in Islamic Thought and Practice* (Cambridge: Cambridge University Press, 2013).

21. Sunnis constitute roughly ninety percent of the world Muslim population, South Asians roughly thirty percent.

22. Theologian Ary A. Roest Crollius notes, "There is perhaps no Scrip-

ture that is so totally a Book of Prayer as is the Qur'an" in "The Prayer of the Qur'an," *Studia Missionalia* 24 (1975): 223.

23. I am very grateful to Peter Cole, Marianna Klar, Joseph Lowry, Nora Schmid, Devin Stewart, Asiya Toorawa, Maryam Toorawa, and Parvine Toorawa for astute feedback on this Introduction.

TRANSLITERATION OF ARABIC

I use a simplified transliteration for Arabic words for readers new to the sounds of Arabic: I use the symbol ' to represent the letter *hamzah*, the symbol ' to represent the letter '*ayn*, and circumflexes for long vowels. Thus, *shahâdah* is pronounced sha-*haa*-dah, Khadîjah is pronounced Kha-*dee*-jah, and *rasûl* is pronounced ra-*sool*.

I do not use circumflexes to show long vowels on words that have entered the English language, such as Allah (*allâh*), Hadith (*hadîth*), Islam (*islâm*), and Qur'an (*qur'ân*). They should be pronounced Al-*laah*, Ha-*deeth*, Is-*laam*, and Qur-*aan*.

Surah (pronounced *soo*-rah), the term for a Qur'anic "chapter," has also entered common English usage, but not *âyah*, the term for a Qur'anic "verse." I use surah, which I capitalize when naming a particular surah, and I use verse and *âyah* interchangeably.

CITING THE QUR'AN

I refer to the Arabic names of surahs the way most English-speaking Muslims do, thus Surah Baqarah (as opposed to the Arabic *Sûrat al-Baqarah*). When I cite a verse or range of verses, I use the Arabic name, followed by the surah number and verse numbers, for example, Baqarah 2:185–86. When I cite only part of a verse, I place a prime after the verse number: 21:87'.

NAMES

Whenever possible, I use the common English name for an individual: Abraham (for Ibrâhîm) and Moses (for Mûsâ). I omit—but regard as implicit—the phrases uttered out of reverence after the mention of God (*ta 'âlâ,* "Exalted," and *'azza wa-jalla,* "Almighty and Majestic"), after the name Muhammad (*sallallâhu 'alayhi wa-sallam,* "may God bless and cherish him"), and after the names of prophets and archangels (*'alayhis-salâm,* "upon whom peace").

DATES

For simplicity, I use Common Era dates.

VERSE MARKERS

As it is customary to print *âyah* numbers, I indicate every tenth *âyah* in the right margin; in the case of longer surahs, I also mark *âyah* divisions with the ◆ symbol.

TERMS

Terms are defined in the Glossary, but I highlight here some of the more important ones:

Qur'an	the revealed Word of God, as transmitted by the Archangel Gabriel to Muhammad (d. 632)
mus'haf	a bound or printed copy of the whole Qur'an
dhikr	measured repetition of Qur'an or pious expressions of praise

du 'â	a supplication or petition to God
salât	the ritual prayer
khutbah	a sermon, delivered on Fridays and on the two Eids, as part of the congregational prayers
wazîfah	a prescribed set of recitations

READING/LISTENING

Muslims do not recite the Qur'an silently; they do so aloud or under their breath, *sotto voce*. These translations are also intended to be read aloud.

The
Devotional
Qur'an

THE FÂTIHAH

ACCORDING TO TRADITION, this early surah was one of the first to be revealed in its entirety. It is called *al-fâtihah*, literally "The Opener," because it is recited first in most devotional practices, and because it appears at the very beginning of the *mus'haf*, that is, the written Qur'an. It is sometimes referred to as *umm al-kitâb*, "The essence of the Book." Imâm 'Alî—the Prophet Muhammad's cousin, later his son-in-law, the first Shi'ite imam, the fourth Sunni caliph, and a paragon of eloquence and piety—is reported to have said that the whole of the Qur'an is contained in the Fâtihah; that is, that its worth and reward are equivalent to the whole Qur'an.

According to a famous hadith, when the Prophet once told a man that he would teach him the greatest surah, he taught him the Fâtihah. And one early Qur'an commentator notes that Satan felt afraid on only four occasions: when he was cursed by God, when he was expelled from Heaven, when Muhammad was sent as a messenger, and when the Fâtihah was revealed.

Unarguably the most important devotional surah, the Fâtihah is also invariably the first to be memorized. It is recited in every cycle of the ritual prayer, thus minimally seventeen times a day; before most devotional practices; at bedtime; and at the graveside. The surah is also sometimes referred to as the "healing surah" (*sûrat al-shifâ '*): a mother might, for instance, recite it and then blow gently on an ailing or agitated infant's face. It is recited by disputing parties when they reach an agreement. It is also recited on festive occasions, including engagements and weddings, and before embarking on a new business enterprise. When food is distributed to the poor, to neighbors, and to relatives on the anniversary of someone's passing, as happens in some cultures, the food item is referred to as *fâtihah*, because the recipient will recite the Fâtihah as a pious act for the benefit of the departed.

In the Name of God
Ever Compassionate and Full of Compassion

Praise God, Lord of all Creation
Ever Compassionate and Full of Compassion
Master of Judgment Day—

You Alone we beseech
and to You Alone we pray

Guide us to the right Path
the Path of those who please You
not of those who earn Your wrath
or who have gone astray

Amen

THE SHORT SURAHS

THE FÂTIHAH MUST BE FOLLOWED in every cycle of the daily ritual prayers by a passage from the Qur'an. This can be a passage of three verses, one long verse, or, as is often the case, a short surah. Since the ritual prayer consists of two, three, or four cycles, ideally at least four surahs should be memorized. Worshipers are at liberty to pick any surahs (or passages) for recitation but often choose one of the last twenty-two short surahs.

The first five verses of Surah 'Alaq (The Clot, 96) are widely held to be the very first lines of Qur'anic revelation conveyed by the Archangel Gabriel to the Prophet Muhammad. This first encounter between angel and prophet is vividly described in the Hadith and in the biographical literature about the Prophet.

Muslims who do not have the whole surah memorized do typically know these five opening verses.

Surah Qadr (Awe, 97) has a special status because it describes the night on which the Qur'an was revealed, which is understood to mean either revelation in its entirety to humanity or the very first instance of revelation to the Prophet Muhammad. According to several hadiths, this occurred on one of the last ten nights of Ramadan. This surah is accordingly recited very frequently in Ramadan.

Surah Zalzalah (Convulsion, 99) is the surah the Prophet Muhammad recommended to an elderly man who asked for a surah that would be all-encompassing, on account of his difficulty reciting for long at his advanced age.

The four shortest surahs in the Qur'an are ʿAsr (Declining Day, 103), Kawthar (Abundance, 108), Nasr (Victory, 110), and Ikhlâs (Sincere Belief, 112). They are therefore often among the earliest surahs memorized and most frequently recited in the ritual prayers. Surah Nasr is widely held to be the last surah revealed to the Prophet Muhammad, some months before his death in 632.

Surahs Kâfirûn (Disbelievers, 109), Ikhlâs (Sincere Belief, 112), Falaq (Daybreak, 113), and Nâs (Humanity, 114) all begin with the word *qul* (literally "Say"), and are therefore sometimes collectively referred to as "the four *quls*." These surahs, which are very short and easy to commit to memory, are said to confer protection from all manner of worldly and otherworldly harm on the reciter, or on the person on whose behalf they are being

recited. Surahs Falaq (113) and Nâs (114) are specifically re-
ferred to as "the two protecting surahs" (*al-mu'awwidhatân*).
Of Surah Falaq (113), the Prophet Muhammad said, "Recite
Surah Falaq—there is no surah you can recite that is as loved
and as speedily accepted by God as this one." In another hadith,
he refers to Surahs Falaq (113) and Nâs (114) as unparalleled in
beauty and excellence. Of Surah Ikhlâs (112), he is reported to
have said, "Everything has a light, and the light of the Qur'an
is Surah Ikhlâs," and to have regarded it as equivalent to a third
of the Qur'an. He enjoined believers to recite these three su-
rahs three times morning and night, saying, "This is sufficient
for you in all respects."

Parents and caregivers will often read "the four *quls*" to and
with their children at bedtime. They are also recited as part of
the ritual invocation over the dead before they are to be buried.
They are often to be found reproduced together on embroi-
dered wall hangings or printed on posters and stickers.

In some parts of the world, the clusters of surahs 95–114, or
surahs 105–14, are recited in the nighttime Ramadan *tarâwîh*
ritual prayers. This is in lieu of another common practice in
the *tarâwîh* prayers, namely the recitation of the entire Qur'an
over the course of twenty-seven nights.

In the name of God
ever Compassionate and full of Compassion

By the morning light
  and darkening night

Your Lord has not forsaken you—
  there has been no slight

The Hereafter is far better
  than this first life

Your Lord will lavish bounties on you—
  and you will know delight

Did He not find you orphaned
  and give you respite?

Find you unaware
  and guide you aright?

Find you wanting
  and amply provide?

Do not subjugate orphans
  and do not repudiate those in need

And loudly proclaim
  your Lord's bounties!

(Duhâ, 93)

SOLACE

In the name of God
ever Compassionate and full of Compassion

Didn't I soothe your heart
   when you were down?

Remove the burden
   that weighed you down?

Lighten the load
   that kept you down?

Raise you up
   and bring you renown?

This shall pass.
   This too shall pass.

When your work is done—attend.
   And turn to your Lord.

(Inshirâh, 94)

THE FIG

In the name of God
ever Compassionate and full of Compassion

By the fig and the olive and Mount Sinai
and this city of sanctuary —

We made humans of flawless quality
then subjected them to the lowest depravity

But those who choose faith and charity
will earn a reward that outlasts eternity

What will deceive you now about true piety?
Is not God's Justice the Highest Authority?

(Tîn, 95)

THE CLOT

In the name of God
ever Compassionate and full of Compassion

Proclaim in the name of your Lord
who created Humankind
from a simple clot—

Proclaim: Your Lord is Generous—
through the pen He taught
human beings what they did not know.

And yet they overstep and are arrogant
and think they're self-sufficient
but all will return to God in the end!

◆

Do you not see the man who tried to block
our servant from prayer?   10

Do you see if Our servant is rightly guided
and summons others to be reverent?

Do you see that man who turns and denies?
Doesn't he know that God is watching?

No! We'll seize him if he persists—
seize him by his forelock,
that false and faithless forelock.

Let him call his henchmen—
We shall summon
Our Angels of Havoc!

◆

No! Let him be.
Pay him no mind—

Bow down.
Draw near.

('Alaq, 96)

AWE

In the name of God
ever Compassionate and full of Compassion

We sent it down on the Night of Awe—
   What, you ask, is the Night of Awe?

The Night of Awe is better by far
   than a thousand months or more

A Night when angels and Spirit descend
   charged by their Lord

A Night of peace—
   Peace, till the break of dawn.

(Qadr, 97)

In the name of God
ever Compassionate and full of Compassion

Disbelieving people of scripture and disbelieving
    idolaters would not change their ways until
    clear evidence was brought to their attention —

A Messenger from God, engaged in the recitation
    of pure pages, comprising true affirmations.

Those who'd received scripture were undivided
    till clear evidence came to their attention —

They were commanded to worship only God,
    to offer sincere devotion as people of true faith,

To be constant in Prayer and give freely in charity.
    This is the true declaration of devotion.

Disbelieving people of scripture and disbelieving
    idolaters will forever abide in Hell —
    they are the very worst creation!

Those who believe and perform good deeds
    are the very best creation!

Their Lord rewards them with Gardens of Eden,
    rivers gently flowing, where they will forever abide.

Their Lord is pleased with them and they with Him.
This is vouchsafed to those in awe of their Lord.

(Bayyinah, 98)

CONVULSION

In the name of God
ever Compassionate and full of Compassion

When the earth convulses
    from its very core

When it spews out remnants
    from its every pore

And bewildered people ask
    Why? What for?

That Day, the Almighty shall make the earth reveal
    what He has in store —

People huddled in batches
    will be shown their actions —

Those who've done an iota of good
    shall see it!

And those who've done an iota of ill
    shall see it!

(Zalzalah, 99)

COURSERS

In the name of God
ever Compassionate and full of Compassion

By coursing chargers
and sparkstriking seethers,
by dawnraiders and dustraisers
and battleline breachers
I swear—

Humans are
ungrateful to their Lord.
They know this full well
yet they covet and hoard.

How can they not know
that graves will be disgorged
and deepest secrets disclosed   10
on a Day when all will be known to their Lord!

('Âdiyât, 100)

In the name of God
ever Compassionate and full of Compassion

The Shattering!
What Shattering?
What precisely
is the Shattering?

A day when people
will be like scattered moths
and mountains
will be like carded cloth

And those whose scales are weighty
shall live a life of bliss
but those whose scales are not
will head to the Abyss

10   What precisely is this?
          Inferno!

(Qâriʿah, 101)

VYING

In the name of God
ever Compassionate and full of Compassion

You all are distracted by vying
over what you hoard and save.
Up to the moment you enter your grave!

You soon will know your fate.
Very soon will you know your fate!
If you saw clearly you would know

That you'll soon be looking
at the Inferno with crystal clarity
and soon be queried about your revelries.

(Takâthur, 102)

In the name of God
ever Compassionate and full of Compassion

By the declining day I swear—
there is no hope for Humanity
    except for those who believe
    and engage in charity,
    and those who enjoin truth
    and enjoin tenacity.

('Asr, 103)

SLANDER

In the name of God
ever Compassionate and full of Compassion

A warning to all
who slander and defame,
who spend their time
counting every gain,
who reckon their wealth
means they will live forever!

    Never!

They will be thrown
into The Crushing.
And how will you know The Crushing?
It is fire kindled by God,
enfolding every heart,
encroaching from every part—

    In pillars of encircling fire.

(Humazah, 104)

THE WAR ELEPHANT

In the name of God
ever Compassionate and full of Compassion

Ponder how your Lord dealt
       with the people on elephant back
How He turned their ploy
       into a powerless attack
And smote them
       with a celestial flock
       that hurled down rain
       of clay-baked rock
       and left them
       like a plain of devoured stalks

(Fîl, 105)

THE QURAYSH

In the name of God
ever Compassionate and full of Compassion

Given the pact of the Quraysh
     —the tribe's pact for travel
    in summer and winter—
Have them worship the Lord of this Shrine
     who protects them from hunger
     and shelters them from fright.

                    (Quraysh, 106)

SIMPLE KINDNESS

In the name of God
ever Compassionate and full of Compassion

See how those who deny the Reckoning behave:
they see orphans and push them away,
they do not call for feeding those in need.

Woe to those who pray but do so heedlessly,
who do things for mere show,
who withhold simple kindness and the smallest deed.

(Mâ'ûn, 107)

ABUNDANCE

In the name of God
ever Compassionate and full of Compassion

On you I lavished
       a heavenly spring.

Worship me,
       make an offering.

Who reviles you
       is bereft and wanting!

(Kawthar, 108)

DISBELIEVERS

In the name of God
ever Compassionate and full of Compassion

Answer—

You who disbelieve!
I do not worship what you worship.
You will not worship what I worship.
Nor will I worship what you worship.

You will not worship what I worship.
Go your way,
I'll go mine.

(Kâfirûn, 109)

VICTORY

In the name of God
ever Compassionate and full of Compassion

When God is victorious and prevails—
when you see throngs embarking on His path—
invoke your Lord with highest praise
    and seek His grace.

    He is ever Clement.

(Nasr, 110)

PALM FIBER

In the name of God
ever Compassionate and full of Compassion

Abû Lahab and his power will shrivel and expire
and not be saved by wealth or profits he might acquire.
He will be cast into a flaming fire!

And his woman—who hauls the kindling—
will soon be haltered in a rope of twisted fiber!

(Masad, 111)

SINCERE BELIEF

In the name of God
ever Compassionate and full of Compassion

Declare—
God is Peerless
God is Flawless
Unbegetting and birthless
Without any partner—Matchless

(Ikhlâs, 112)

DAYBREAK

In the name of God
ever Compassionate and full of Compassion

Repeat—I seek refuge in the Lord of the Daybreak
　　From the evil He has made,
　　From the evil of nightgloom when it drapes,
　　From the evil of sorceresses spitting on knots,
　　And from the evil of the envier when he plots.

(Falaq, 113)

HUMANITY

In the name of God
ever Compassionate and full of Compassion

Repeat—I seek refuge in the Lord of Humanity,
Sovereign over Humanity, God for all Humanity,
  From the evil of the Whisperer's calumny—
  Insinuating in the hearts
  Of Jinn and Humanity.

(Nâs, 114)

ÂYAT AL-KURSÎ

ÂYAT AL-KURSÎ, ALSO WIDELY KNOWN as The Throne Verse—though strictly *kursî* is a reference to the pedestal on which the throne rests, rather than the throne itself—is according to one hadith the greatest verse in the Qur'an. In another hadith, the Prophet Muhammad says that it is equivalent to a quarter of the Qur'an, and in another, that anyone who recites the first three verses of Surah Baqarah (The Cow, 2), followed by Âyat al-Kursî and the last three verses of Surah Baqarah, will never forget the Qur'an.

This verse is one of the very first Qur'anic passages memorized by Muslims. When recited before sleep, it keeps one's home and family safe. Reciting it at any time is said to protect one from harm. A written version is accordingly worn by some

Muslims as an amulet or on a pendant and frequently graces people's homes and workplace on framed calligraphy, tilework, or even simple adhesive stickers. When recited after each of the daily ritual prayers, it is said to pave the way to paradise.

THE THRONE VERSE

God—There is no God but
He, without beginning or end,
Unwearying, untouched by Time,
Keeper of Heaven and Earth,
Unattainable without permission,
Knower of what is and was
   —others know only what He allows.
Heaven and Earth are subsumed by His
   Throne and are preserved without effort.
God—Exalted, Sublime.

(Baqarah 2:255)

SURAH YÂ SÎN

JUST AS THE FÂTIHAH and Âyat al-Kursî are central to Muslim devotion, so too is Surah Yâ Sîn (36). In one hadith, the Prophet Muhammad says, "Everything has a core—the core of the Qur'an is Yâ Sîn." It is reported in another hadith that reciting it earns the same reward as reciting the entire Qur'an ten times, and that the surah itself will intercede on Judgment Day on behalf of the reciter. For this reason, Yâ Sîn is often the one long surah Muslims memorize and the one they read before or after their daily ritual prayers. Even those who have not memorized it can typically follow along when they hear it recited.

Yâ Sîn is recited to those who are on their deathbeds, at the graveside, and for the departed. Yâ Sîn is also recited to ward off ill. It is often reproduced alone in small booklets that can be carried on one's person for pious distribution—the reward then accrues to the reciter, to the departed in whose name the booklet is produced, and to the producer of the booklet.

In the name of God, ever Compassionate and full of Compassion

By Yâ Sîn, and this discerning Recitation, I bear witness ◆ That you are indeed one of Our messengers ◆ sent on a straight path ◆ That this is Revelation from the Almighty, full of Mercy and Kindness ◆ With which to warn a people whose ancestors went unwarned and who now are heedless. ◆ The verdict is punishment for their faithlessness. ◆ We have placed iron collars around their necks and yoked them beneath their chins so that their heads are pushed up and motionless ◆ and placed barriers in front of them and barriers behind, and enveloped them, so they cannot see. ◆ It's all the same to them, whether you warn them or not: they will never profess. ◆ You can only warn the ones who heed the Reminder and who fear the Ever Compassionate, even though they cannot see Him. To such believers, give assurances of generous reward and forgiveness. ◆ The power to bring the dead to life rests with Us. We record the deeds they performed and the legacy they leave behind. And We take account of everything in a Register that is crystal clear.

◆

Give them the example of the city—messengers were sent to its populace. ◆ When two were sent, they were turned away, so We reinforced them with a third. The three then repeated, *God has sent us.* ◆ But the people said, *You are men just like us. The Ever*

Compassionate has not sent anything. Your words are false. ◆ *Our Lord knows we have been sent to you,* they replied, *Our duty is to convey a warning clear and obvious.* ◆ But the people said, *For us, your presence is inauspicious—* ◆ *If you do not stop immediately, we will stone you and inflict painful punishment.* ◆ *Keep your omen for yourselves,* the messengers replied. *Do you say this because you have been reminded? You surely transgress!* ◆

20 Then a man came running from the far side of the city, saying, *My people, follow the messengers,* ◆ *Follow those who offer a warning, asking for nothing in return, who are rightly guided and pious.* ◆ *Why would I not worship the One who created me and to Whom you shall all return regardless.* ◆ *Instead of Him, do you expect me to worship idols? If the Ever Compassionate wishes me harm, their alleged intercession will be worthless.* ◆ *They will not be able to save me—* ◆ *if I did worship them, my error would be grievous!* ◆ *Messengers, I believe in your Lord! My people, heed my advice!* ◆

Enter Paradise, We said to him, and he exclaimed, *If only my people knew how my Lord has forgiven me and included me among the righteous.* ◆ We sent no heavenly army against his people after him. We did not need to.— ◆ One Blast is enough for them to be rendered lifeless.

◆

30 Disgraceful Humanity! Mocking every messenger! ◆ Does it not see how many preceding generations We destroyed,

generations that will never come again? ◆ Every single one of them will be gathered for judgment before Us. ◆

The dead Earth is a sign for them: ◆ We bring it to life and produce grain from it for them to eat as they please. ◆ We have made springs gush in gardens of vines and in oases of palm trees ◆ so they can enjoy their fruits. Their hands did not produce this artistry! Will they persist in being thankless? ◆ Glory to God who created in pairs the yield of the earth, humanity itself, and other creations of which they are oblivious. ◆

And the night is a sign for them: We strip the Day from it, and suddenly they are in darkness. ◆ This is the decree of the Almighty, the Omniscient—that the Sun hastens to its resting-place. ◆ And We have apportioned phases for the Moon, until it wanes like a spike of dates, withered and sapless. ◆ The Sun is 40 unable to pass the Moon, and the Night unable to outpace the Day: each travels in its own orbit. ◆

A sign for them, too, is that We brought their progeny into the Ark, ◆ That We created other vessels, of like purpose, for their journey. ◆ If We wished, We could drown them— ◆ There would be no one to help and no one to save them, except through Our forgiveness, which would offer a short respite. ◆

When they are told, *Beware the dangers of this world before you, and beware of what comes Next, so that you may be spared*, they are heedless. ◆ Every one of the Lord's numerous signs presented them they reject as worthless. ◆

When they are told, *Spend of what God has given you*, the unbelievers say to the pious, ◆ *Why should we feed those whom God feeds? Your error is clear and obvious.* ◆ *If what you say about the Last Day is true, when will that promise be kept—tell us?* ◆ They will not have to wait for anything but a single Blast, and while they are
50 busy haggling, it will knock them senseless ◆ They will have no time to reach home, to bequeath what they possess! ◆ The Blast will sound and they will surge from their graves into their Lord's presence, and say ◆ *What! Who has roused us from our sleep? This must be the Day the messengers affirmed, the Day the Ever Compassionate promised us . . .* ◆ A single Blast will gather them before Us. ◆

That Day, no soul will be shown the least injustice: ◆ Your deeds will determine the reward We give. ◆ That Day, the Garden dwellers will be busy in their joyousness. ◆ They and their spouses will recline on couches, in shade and coolness. ◆ They will have fruits and whatever they request in abundance. ◆ The Ever Compassionate will greet them with a salutation of peace,
60 ◆ And He will say, *Sinners, this Day, stand apart!* ◆ *Children of Adam, did We not charge you not to obey Satan, your avowed enemy,* ◆ *to obey and worship Us* ◆ *that this is the path, straight and errorless?* ◆ *And yet, he has led a great many of you astray—could you not recognize this?* ◆ *This is the Hell you were promised:* ◆ *embrace it now, for you were faithless.* ◆

That Day, We shall seal their disbelieving lips and render them speechless. ◆ Their hands will recount their deeds, their feet will bear witness. ✦ If We wished, We could have blotted out their eyes, and forced them to grope for the path. ✦ But then how would they see this Day, and bear witness? ✦ And if We wished, We could have paralyzed them where they stood, unable either to move back or to progress. ✦ Those We've allowed to grow old, We can make ageless. ✦ Can they not see this?

✦

We have not taught him poetry and verse—that is below his status. ✦ This revelation is simply a Reminder and Recitation, clear and luminous ✦ with which to warn the living, and to justify punishment for the faithless. ✦ 70

Do the unbelievers not see that We fashioned the livestock they possess, ✦ that We have made animals for their profit, ✦ to ride, and eat, from which to draw milk and other benefit? Still are they thankless? ✦ Still they forsake God, worshiping false gods, hoping for their aid and buttress. ✦ They will not be able to help, and will instead be like a hostile force. ✦ So do not let their words affect you—We know what they keep in their hearts, and what they openly express.

✦

Does Humanity not see that We created it from a simple drop of semen? And yet, it is brazenly contentious! ✦ Forgetting its origin, it challenges by asking, *Who can revive bones decayed and lifeless?* ✦ Answer thus: *The One who created them in the first place*

will revive them, the One who has knowledge of creation and all it
80 *encompasses,* ◆ *the One who gave you the gift of fire from greenest trees,* ◆ *for you to ignite as you please.* ◆ Can the one who created heaven and earth not create others like them? Of course! He is the real and All-Knowing Creator. ◆ When He wills a thing he says *"Be!"* and it is! ◆

To Him the glory, in Whose grasp is true dominion, and to Whom you will all return as He decrees.

SURAHS FOR DAILY
AND WEEKLY RECITATION

MUSLIMS CAN READ OR RECITE any portion of the Qur'an as an act of worship and devotion. Some read a little, some a lot, some occasionally, some every day. In a widely cited hadith, the Prophet Muhammad says that whoever reads even just one letter of one word will be rewarded tenfold.

Devout Muslims aspire to complete at least one full reading (*khatm*) of the Qur'an; in many cultures, when a child finishes a *khatm* for the first time, the family will celebrate the occasion with gifts and acts of charity. Many Muslims read the Qur'an cover to cover more than one time and aspire to complete a full reading in however long it takes, or within a year, or in a month (during Ramadan, for example); some do so in a week, or even as little as three days. To facilitate this, printed Qur'ans (and Qur'an apps) are divided into thirty equal parts. Each part, or *juz'*, is then further subdivided into four equal quarters, al-lowing the reader or reciter to plan easily for installments of 30, 60, 120, or 240. The Qur'an is also divided into 540 "para-graphs" of differing lengths, called *rukû'*, which some readers and reciters prefer to use as a division.

In addition to reading fixed portions of the Qur'an, one might choose in addition, or instead, to establish regular devo-tions. Just as there are surahs recommended for the ritual prayer and specifically for Friday, there are also surahs and passages and verses recommended for daily, nightly, and weekly recita-tion, based either on the practice of the Prophet Muhammad or on the practice of other pious figures such as the Prophet's Companions, the Shiite Imams, learned religious scholars, or Sufi masters.

For this volume, I have selected—in addition to Surah Yâ Sîn (36) above and Surah Kahf (The Cave, 18) below—five of the most widely recited, memorized, and beloved surahs:

Surah Naba' (The Great News, 78): The Prophet Muham-mad said this was one of the surahs that turned his hair gray, an indication not only of its portentous message but also of his frequent recitation of it.

Surah Wâqi'ah (The Inevitable, 56): According to the Prophet Muhammad, whoever recites this surah every night shall never be afflicted by need.

Surah Mulk (The Kingdom, 67): Of this surah, the Prophet Muhammad said, "I would dearly love for it to be in the heart of everyone in my community." He also said it would intercede on behalf of the reciter on Judgment Day.

Surah Rahmân (The Ever Compassionate, 55): The Prophet Muhammad said, "Everything has an adornment—the Qur'an's adornment is Surah Rahmân."

Surah Insân (Humankind, 76): The Prophet Muhammad would recite this surah in the predawn *fajr* prayer; the reward for reciting it, he said, is Paradise.

In the name of God
ever Compassionate and full of Compassion

What are they asking
each other about?
About the Great News
over which they're falling out?
They'll soon know all.
Soon they'll know.
Very soon.

Didn't We make—
the earth a place for rest?
The mountains like pegs?
Didn't We create you in pairs
And give you the gift of sleep?
Provide night as a shroud?
And day for toil?

Didn't we fashion the seven heavens
and cause a Lamp to shine?
Cause clouds brimful with rain
to saturate every garden
and bring forth fruit and grain?

The Day of Decision is Ours to dictate!
When the Blast sounds, you'll huddle

as the heavens open their gates
and mountains melt away. 20

Hell will be lying in wait!
A weak retreat, hardly an escape!
where sinners will for ages abide
without refreshment
or coolness to quench their thirst,
only scalding water and pus.
A fitting recompense!

They didn't believe Our Account
and called our revelations lies.
We have recorded it all in a Writ!
Taste now the growing torment
—that is all We'll allow! 30

The righteous, however, will reap
the finest reward—vineyards and gardens,
ageless and lissome companions
and brimming cups.
No false claims or idle talk.
This is your Lord's compensation,
a fitting reward
by the Compassionate Lord
of heaven and earth
whom none will be able to question!

That Day when Spirit and angels

will all stand straight,
when just those permitted
shall speak, and speak true,
a Day of Truth!

Whoever wishes should make
His Lord his ultimate end.

We've warned you—
40 of looming punishment that day,
when good people will see
what they have wrought
and disbelievers will cower and say
I wish I were nothing—
Nothing but dust!

(Naba', 78)

In the name of God
ever Compassionate and full of Compassion

When the Inevitable happens
—and none can deny it will—
raising high and casting out

When the land is ravaged by tremors
and the mountains shattered
and scattered about

You will be in three companies—

The Companions of the Right?
   Oh, those companions of the Right!

The Companions of the Left?
   Woe for those companions of the Left!

And the Surpassing—surpassing all!—   10
   will be in God's close company
   in Gardens of felicity,
   some from distant times,
   a few from more recently

   Gazing at one another
   on jeweled beds of gold,
   served cups of nectar

by ageless youths —
ambrosia's decanter,
carafes of innocuous wine,
20   any fruit at their beck and call,
any fowl or flesh at all,
and dark-eyed girls
like hidden pearls.

All this a reward for their deeds,
no empty words or blasphemy,
only tender words of peace.

◆

The Companions of the Right
    —blessed companions these!—

Will be in groves of thornless lote trees
and clustered acacias

30   In boundless shade,
fountains brimming over,
any fruit in season
ripe and free to taste

Beds raised high,
and ideal virgin companions
of exclusive creation,
eternally young, devoted.

All this favor for
the Companions of the Right!
Some from distant times
some from more recently.

◆

The Companions of the Left
—wretched companions these!—
Will be in scalding water
and scorching storm,
blackest smoke their only shade,
uncooling and unkind.

They basked once in luxury,
unhinged in their transgression
and asked in mockery
"When we are bones and dust
will we be brought back to life?
Our fathers, and theirs too?"

Reply—Yes!
Those from distant times
and from more recently.
You who deny and go astray
will all be gathered on an appointed Day
and devour the fruit of Zaqqûm
until your stomachs are bloated
and lap at scalding water

like parched camels—
such hospitality on the Day of Doom!

◆

We created you—will you not concede this?

The seed you discharge—
Have you created that, or have We?

60 Your death We decreed!
You will not impede Us
from changing you
to a form unknown to you.
Recall that you were created once—
Still, won't you take heed?

The seeds you sow—
Do you produce that harvest, or do We?

We could turn it to chaff if We wished
and you would lament:
*"We are in debt, with nothing to show
for what we've grown."*

The water you drink—
Do you rain it down, or do We?

70 We could make it brackish, if We wished.
Still, you will not give thanks!

The fire you light—
Is it you who produce the kindling, or do We?

  Let it be a reminder of Our sovereignty,
  provision for those who travel the desert at night.

    Praise the Name of God Almighty!

        ◆

I swear by the constellations
—a powerful oath if only you knew—
  that this is a sublime Recitation,
  guarded within a Book,
  conveyed by the pure alone,
  a Revelation from   80
  The Lord of Creation.

Is it this Word you despise?
Do you requite Us with nothing but lies?
Why do you look on helpless
when you hear the rattling of death?
We are far closer then,
though you cannot see Us.
If you think yourselves exempt
make good on your claim
and try to restore your soul to its frame.

If that soul is destined for God's company
then rest it will be—fragrance and gardens of serenity.

90 If for the company of the Right
greetings from those Companions.

And if for deniers gone astray
then let scaldwater be their hospitality
and Hellfire too.

This is Truth. And Certainty.
Praise His Name Almighty!

(Wâqiʿah, 56)

THE KINGDOM

In the name of God
ever Compassionate and full of Compassion

Hallowed be
the One who holds the Kingdom
the One with absolute Power—

who created Death
as well as Life as a test

to show whose deeds are worthier:
the Lord Almighty, the Forgiver—

who created the Seven Heavens
layered one upon the other.

You will find no rupture
in His design!
Can you see the smallest fissure? Look!

Look again! And again!
Your vision will only weaken,
grow dreary and darken.

◆

With lightbursts we've adorned the Firmament
to drive out demons destined for the Fire
and torment prepared for those

who reject their Lord—
a truly gruesome predicament . . .

Cast into the seething cauldron
they will hear it roil and smolder
and all but overspill with furor.
Hell's Guardians will question them:
Weren't you sent a Warning?

A Warner did come, they'll say, *but we were in denial.*
We said: God revealed to us nothing whatsoever!
We said: You're utterly deluded!
10 *If only we'd listened and understood*
We wouldn't be inmates now of the Fire!

Though they confess their sins—
Away with these Friends of the Fire!

◆

And those awed by an unseen Lord
will know forgiveness and a great reward.

What your hearts conceal He sees
whether it's hidden or revealed.

Subtle in Knowing's grace,
how could He not know His creation?

It's He who made the Earth tractable to you.
So travel its byways, partake of its bounties.

In the end Resurrection will come.

Are you certain the One in Heaven
won't make the earth give way beneath you
in a great convulsion?

Are you certain the One in Heaven
will not unleash a windstorm of stones?

> Maybe then you'll grasp
> how grim is Our Admonition!

◆

Those who came before them
were in denial as well—Our response was swift.

Don't they see the birds above them
with wings folded or outspread?

The Lord of Mercy alone can hold them aloft.
He watches over all that exists.

What army could defend you, apart from the Lord of Mercy?   20
Those who disbelieve are deluded, and drift.

And who else could provide if He withholds provision?
They flee, willfully, from the Truth.

Who is guided rightly?
He who grovels face down

or he who walks the Straight Path
upright and mindful?

Tell them: It is He who fashioned you,
who granted you hearing, sight, and mind.
And yet you are scarcely thankful.

Tell them: It is He who dispersed you on earth.
Before Him will you all be mustered.

And still they ask: *When will this all come true,
if you are being truthful?*

Tell them: That knowledge remains with God alone:
I simply bring you the Warning.

The disbelievers' faces will twist
With grief when they see it close at hand.

And they will be reminded:
Isn't this what you were promised?

◆

Say to them: Consider this—
whether God destroys
me and those with me,
whether He shows us His mercy,
who will save the disbelievers
from a painful agony?

Say to them: He is Full of Grace.
We believe in Him alone,
and in Him we place our trust.
You will all soon know
who has clearly gone astray.

Say to them: Consider this—   30
who will provide you
with flowing water
if all your waters
sink into the clay?

(Mulk, 67)

In the name of God
ever Compassionate and full of Compassion

The Ever Compassionate
taught the Recitation
created Humanity
and taught it Clear Expression

The Sun and Moon follow a fixed rotation
and plants and trees prostrate in adoration

He raised the skies
and balanced everything in true proportion
so that you not disturb the proportion:
Be fair in your estimation
and do not skew the proportion

He established the Earth for His creation
bearing fruit and fronded palms
aromatics and huskèd grain—

which then of your Lord's wonders
do you both deny in vain?

He fashioned humans from clay, like an earthenware jar
and fashioned jinns from smokeless fire—

which then
of your Lord's wonders

10

do you both
deny in vain?

Lord of both risings and both settings—

which then of your Lord's wonders
do you both deny in vain?

He brings fresh water and salt water together
But they do not overrun, a barrier remains—   20

which then
of your Lord's wonders
do you both
deny in vain?

Both waters contain coral and pearls—

which then of your Lord's wonders
do you both deny in vain?

The fording ships, like towering ridges in the seas,
are part of His domain

which then
of your Lord's wonders
do you both
deny in vain?

Everything on the Earth shall wane
except the countenance of your Lord

full of Majesty, Magnanimous:
It alone shall remain—

which then of your Lord's wonders
do you both deny in vain?

Everyone on earth and in the heavens beseeches Him
all matters are His, daily to ordain—

30

which then
of your Lord's wonders
do you both
deny in vain?

We shall soon have dealings
with both you wearisome legions!—

which then of your Lord's wonders
do you both deny in vain?

Assembly of jinns and humans
if you can venture beyond
the regions of Heaven and Earth, do so:
You shall through Divine power
and permission alone—

which then
of your Lord's wonders
do you both
deny in vain?

Smokeless flames and flaming smoke
will descend on you
you will have no protection—

which then of your Lord's wonders
do you both deny in vain?

When the skies are torn apart
and look like hide dyed crimson—

which then
of your Lord's wonders
do you both
deny in vain?

That day, neither human nor jinn
will be questioned about their transgression—

which then of your Lord's wonders   40
do you both deny in vain?

The guilty shall be known by distinguishing marks
and seized by foot and forelock—

which then
of your Lord's wonders
do you both
deny in vain?

This will be that Hell-Fire
denied by those bearing blame

who'll run back and forth between
a roiling Cauldron and the flames—

which then of your Lord's wonders
do you both deny in vain?

But for those who fear standing
before their Lord, a pair of Gardens—

which then
of your Lord's wonders
do you both
deny in vain?

With myriad branching trees therein—

which then of your Lord's wonders
do you both deny in vain?

Two springs flowing in each domain—

which then
of your Lord's wonders
do you both
deny in vain?

And in each place two
of every fruit and every description—

which then of your Lord's wonders
do you both deny in vain?

All within reach of the righteous
reclined on divans of silk brocade —

which then
of your Lord's wonders
do you both
deny in vain?

Companions of modest gaze and virginal, residing there
untouched before by human or jinn —

which then of your Lord's wonders
do you both deny in vain?

Like rubies or coral gems of perfection —

which then
of your Lord's wonders
do you both
deny in vain?

Can the reward for Right Action be aught   60
but Right Action? —

which then of your Lord's wonders
do you both deny in vain?

And beyond these, two Gardens again —

which then
of your Lord's wonders

do you both
deny in vain?

Dense with dark vegetation—

which then of your Lord's wonders
do you both deny in vain?

With two springs that surge
and which nothing could constrain—

which then
of your Lord's wonders
do you both
deny in vain?

Pomegranates, date palms, and fruit of the heavens—

which then of your Lord's wonders
do you both deny in vain?

Virtuous, lovely companions within—

which then
of your Lord's wonders
do you both
deny in vain?

Dark-eyed beauties in secluded pavilions—

which then of your Lord's wonders
do you both deny in vain?

70

Untouched by jinns or humans—

which then
of your Lord's wonders
do you both
deny in vain?

The righteous recline there
on mottled carpets and green cushions—

Which then of your Lord's wonders
do you both deny in vain?

Your Lord
Full of Majesty, Magnanimous!

Blessèd
be His name!

(Rahmân, 55)

HUMANKIND

In the name of God
ever Compassionate and full of Compassion

Has there not been a time
when humans were nothing to speak of?

We created them from a drop of sperm
We tested them and made them see and hear

And We guided them along the path
whether or not they heeded Our favor

◆

For unbelievers We have prepared
shackles and manacles and a blazing fire

But the righteous shall drink
a wine blended with camphor

Those devoted to God imbibe
from a gushing fountain, at their pleasure

Fulfilling their vows and fearing a Day
whose calamity shall spread far

Feeding, for the love of God,
captive, orphan, and pauper

Saying, *"We feed you for the sake of God alone*

seeking neither thanks nor reward

We fear of our Lord
a Day of excruciating anger"

But God will shield them from that calamity
and immerse them in delight and splendor

And for their constancy reward them
with a Garden and garments of silken fiber

They will recline on thrones and notice
neither fiery heat nor frigid winter

The garden's humble shadows will shade them
the boughs of fruit bowed low and humbled

Among them shall be passed
goblets of crystal and vessels of silver

Silvery crystal from which to help
themselves at leisure

And a wine blended with ginger
a mixture ethereal

Flowing from a fountain called
Salsabîl

About them shall roam eternal youths
who'll seem like scattered pearls

Seeing them, you would behold such grace
in a realm of such grandeur

Their tunics gold and green silk brocade
their arms bedecked in bracelets of silver

Their Lord shall give them a draught
of a spirit that's pure

All this is your reward—
worthy is your endeavor!

We have sent the Qur'an down
gradually

Forbear, and obey your Lord's commands
yield not to the sinner or disbeliever

Morning and evening, the name of your Lord
recite and remember

Glorify Him the whole night through
and for part of it prostrate to Him

Others love the fleeting world
and ignore a Day of great burden

We created them and made them strong
We could exchange them for others like them
if We wished . . .

This is an admonition!

Take a straight path to the Lord
whosoever will

But remember that none of you can   30
will without God's will

God knows all

He admits to His mercy
whomever He wishes

For those who do wrong
he has readied painful torment

(Insân, 76)

FRIDAY VERSES AND SURAHS

THE FRIDAY CONGREGATIONAL PRAYER (*salât al-jumu'ah*, commonly Jummah)—and also the congregational prayers on the high holidays, Eid al-Fitr and Eid al-Adha—effectively consists of two parts, the *khutbah*, or sermon, and the ritual prayer. The *khutbah* is delivered by a *khatîb*, or sermon-giver, usually from a raised *minbar*, or pulpit, facing the congregation. The sermon can be individually composed, extemporized, taken from a book of sermons, or, as is the case in some countries, imposed by a central religious authority. The sermon consists of exhortations, often reprising and relying on passages in the Qur'an and hadith corpus, about belief, religious practice, and justice; and of supplications, again, either individually composed or from the Qur'an. The *khutbah* can also include calls to action and critiques of social ills.

The six Qur'anic passages included here are routinely included in the *khutbah* and are among the most widely known and cited verses in the Qur'an. Because congregants hear these verses every week at the Friday prayers (or on radio or television, as the *khutbah* from the principal mosque in many capitals and major cities is broadcast live), they often have them memorized.

Surahs A'lâ (The Most High, 87) and Ghâshiyah (The Enfoldment, 88) are the two surahs the Prophet Muhammad favored for recitation in the Friday (and Eid) prayers. Of Surah Kahf (The Cave, 18), the Prophet Muhammad said that whoever recites the ten opening *âyahs* or the ten closing ones will be protected against al-Dajjâl, the Antichrist. The reading of Surah Kahf is highly recommended from after the sunset *maghrib* ritual prayer on Thursday night until the sunset prayer on Friday.

God commands justice, and kindness,
    and benevolence to kin.
He forbids indecency, oppression,
    and transgression.
He offers you counsel—

    Take heed.

(Nahl 16:90)

Remember Me—
I shall remember you.

Be grateful to Me
and do not deny Me.

(Baqarah 2:152)

"CALL ON ME—I WILL ANSWER"

Call on Me —
I will answer

(Ghâfir 40:60')

Believers, be mindful of God,
    and be forthright in your speech.

God will set your actions right
    and wipe out your misdeeds—

Those who obey God and His Emissary
    achieve a great Victory!

(Ahzâb 33:70–71)

"BELIEVERS, BE IN AWE OF GOD"

Believers, be in awe of God
   as He merits
And submit to Him
   till your dying breath!

(Âl 'Imrân 3:102)

"GOD AND HIS ANGELS SEND BLESSINGS ON THE PROPHET"

God and His angels send blessings
    on the Prophet—

Believers, invoke your blessings on him
    and offer greetings of peace.

(Ahzâb 33:56)

In the name of God
ever Compassionate and full of Compassion

Honor the Name
    of your Lord Most High!

Who created and gave measure,
    determined, and brought order

Who brings forth green pasture,
    then makes it wither!

We shall teach you to recite
    and not forget, except as God decrees.

He knows what you reveal
    and what you conceal.

We shall ease you into Ease!

◆

Use the Scripture to remind them—
    some may profit from the reminder.   10

It will avail the fearer of God,
    but the wretched shall pass it over—

They shall burn in a Great Fire
    where they shall neither live nor die.

Those who purify themselves and prosper
  shall invoke their Lord and engage in prayer.

Still, it's life in the world you prefer—
  But the Hereafter is infinitely better!

This was made clear in what We already sent you—
  Abraham's Scrolls, and Moses' Scripture.

(A'lâ, 87)

THE ENFOLDMENT

In the name of God
ever Compassionate and full of Compassion

Has word reached you of the Enfoldment?

That Day some faces will be dejected,
    laboring and defeated.
The Fire they enter will be vehement.
    The Fount they drink from—fulminant!
Their only food—thorn and bracken
    that neither satisfies nor fattens.

That Day others will be jubilant,
    content with their efforts,
    recumbent in a lofty Garden,
    free of idle ranting,
    graced with a Fountain overflowing.

The couches there loftily displayed,
    cups carefully conveyed,
    cushions plentifully arrayed,
    carpets beautifully laid.

Do people not wonder
    how camels were fashioned?
    how the high heavens were fastened?
    how the mountains were battened down?
    how the level earth was flattened?

Remind them!
You were sent to remind them
    not to rule and to mind them.

But those who turn away in disbelief
    will receive God's Punishment!

All in the end must return to Us
    and their Reckoning must go through Us.

(Ghâshiyah, 88)

In the name of God,
ever Compassionate and full of Compassion

Praise God who revealed to His servant a Book free of deformity
◆ a Righteous Book with warnings of severe Punishment and
assurances too of a Great Bounty: ◆ Paradise for virtuous
Believers to abide in for Eternity! ◆ A Book warning those who
say that God has progeny! ◆ What do they or their forefathers
know! What they speak is pure Perjury! ◆ If they turn away
and ignore this warning, you might feel consumed by misery. ◆

We fashioned everything on earth as finery and as a test to see
whose deeds are best. ◆ Soon We shall turn the land into barren
dust.

◆

Do you think the Companions of the Cave and Tablet are the
only signs of Our wondrous artistry? ◆ Some youths repaired to ₁₀
a Cave calling out *"Lord, provide us with Guidance in this our
predicament — bestow on us your Clemency!"* ◆ We shielded their
ears and made them sleep for years ◆ then revived them and
watched to see which of the two camps best reckoned how long
they'd slept. ◆

We recount their Story accurately —

The story of youths who believed in their Lord, youths

rewarded with Guidance for their Piety ◆ We bolstered them when they stood firm saying, *"Our Lord is Lord of Heaven and Earth—we shall never call on any other deity! That would be calumny!"* ◆ *"Our people worship idols instead! Can they produce a basis for this, a clear authority! Can anyone be more corrupt than fabricators, opposing God with their iniquity?"* ◆ and when they advised one another: *"And when you have forsworn them and what they worship besides God, let us retreat to a Cave where God shall shower you with His Clemency—In this time of need shall He provide comfort"* ◆

At daybreak you would have seen the sun move past the Cave on the right, at nightfall on the left, while they slept in its cleft—a Sign of God's artistry!

Those God leads are guided right! But for those allowed to stray, there is no guide to show them the Way! ◆

You would have thought them awake but they were deep in sleep—We turned them onto their right and left and their dog stretched his paws to the threshold—If you had looked too closely you would have fled, filled with terror and anxiety ◆

From their slumber we brought them to life and they began to debate: *"How long have we endured like this? A day, part of a day?"* *"Your Lord knows best how long you endured!"* came one answer, *"Send one of your number into town with some silver"* said another *"to seek out fine food and bring it as provision—but* do so discreetly ◆ *If they get wind of you they will stone you and*

20

88

force their beliefs on you—you shall never know prosperity" ◆

But We let them be discovered so that people would learn that God's promise is True—that the Hour is a certainty. They began to argue—Some said, *"Wall them up—Let their Lord take care of them!"* But others prevailed, *"Let's build a house of worship about their company"* ◆

People will say, *"They were three and their dog makes four,"* or, *"Five and their dog makes six"*—guessing ignorantly! They will say, *"Seven and their dog makes eight!"* Tell them, *"The number is known only to my Lord and to a select few,"* and only debate with them ostensibly—Do not solicit views from any about how many! ◆

And remember never to say of a task, *"I shall definitely do this tomorrow"* ◆ without adding *"if God wills."* If you forget, recall God at that very moment and say, *"Perhaps my Lord will guide me to what's right, guide me more steadily"* ◆

They endured three hundred and nine years in their sanctuary ◆ Say, *"God knows best how long they endured—He knows the Unseen in Heaven and on Earth—He sees all, hears all! They have Him alone as Protector and His dominion is subject to Him, and to Him only!"*

◆

Recite what was revealed to you from His Book—None can change His words. There is no refuge but He. ◆ And content yourself with the company of those who praise their Lord morning and night, seeking his Countenance. Do not look beyond them, seeking this fleeting life's finery, and do not heed those whose hearts We made heedless of praise, followers of whims, whose affairs are always in disarray ◆

Affirm — *"Truth comes from your Lord: Let those who wish believe, and those who wish deny this blatantly."* We have prepared an encroaching Fire for the wicked. When they ask for relief, the water shall scald their faces in a downpour like molten copper!

What an awful refreshment, what a wretched amenity! ◆

30 Reward awaits even a solitary deed by those who believe, who act righteously ◆ Gardens of Eden with rivers flowing underfoot. Adorned in bracelets of gold, and arrayed in green silks and brocade, reclined on divans of ornate embroidery!

What a blessed reward, what a beautiful amenity!

◆

Tell them the parable of two men —

To one man we gave two gardens of grapevines flanking fields of crops and surrounded by date palms. Both gardens flourished unabatedly ◆ A stream flowed between them and fruit grew abundantly ◆ The one man addressed the other, *"I have greater riches than you and a stronger community"* ◆ and returned to his estate saying to himself deludedly ◆ *"I do not think this will abate* ◆ *Nor the Last Hour ever come — and even if*

I am returned to my Lord, I am certain it will end happily!" ♦

The other responded, *"Do you deny the One who fashioned you from clay, then semen, into a man?* ♦ *He alone is my Lord and God—I associate no one with His ways* ♦ *If you'd but entered your garden saying 'God's will be done! Strength comes from God alone!' You may deem me inferior in riches and in progeny* ♦ *But it could be my Lord has something better than your estate in store for me. He might send down a thunderbolt and turn your estate* 40 *to dust, instantaneously* ♦ *Or its water might suddenly run into earth and elude you completely"* ♦

And ruin indeed came to the first man's harvest and destroyed it utterly. As his trellises crumbled to the ground he wrung his hands at all he'd spent on them, and could only say, *"If only I'd associated no one with my Lord!"* ♦ But there was no help to be found, no company—there is only God!—so he foundered helplessly ♦ On such a Day succor can come only from the one true God.

From Him come surest Reward and destiny

♦

Tell them the parable of this fleeting life—

It is like the water We send from the skies. The earth's plants absorb it—but they soon turn to chaff in the winds.

Over everything, God exerts full authority ♦ Property and progeny are merely the finery of this fleeting life! Only virtuous deeds abide. For your Lord, these merit reward, these are cause for hope. ◆

Heed the Day We dispatch the mountains and trample the land into clay. We shall gather them, forgetting no one! ◆ They will present in rows, and We will say *"As I once created you, you come to Me! Do you still claim there is no appointed Day?"* ◆ The Ledger shall be brought and the miscreants shall cower at its contents — *"We are done for! What is this Ledger that records every detail great and small, that accurately records it all?"* — It shall be laid out for them! Your Lord treats no one oppressively.

◆

50 When We asked the angels to bow to Adam, they did — not so Iblîs, the jinn who defied his Lord's command. Would you ally yourself to him and his progeny? And not to Me? When they are the enemy? Surely for sinners a wretched deal! ◆ I showed them neither their Creation nor their own generation, and I won't admit perverters to my Company! ◆

Heed the Day when He shall say, *"Call those you claim are associates — associates to Me!"* They will call and get no answer: We will scatter them in an abyss of calamity ◆ Miscreants seeing the Fire will know: they shall find no delivery ◆

We have resorted in this Book to every kind of example, but of all creatures Humans are by far the most refractory ◆ Guidance has come! What prevents them from believing or seeking forgiveness from their Lord? Has the practice of their forefathers swayed them? Would imminent punishment persuade them? ✦ We send good tidings and warning—nothing more—with every Emissary. The disbelievers insist on specious argument to oppose Truth and treat My fair warning as mockery! ✦

Who is more misguided than those who have been reminded, who turn their backs on Our proof, and forget what their hands have wrought? We shroud their hearts lest they understand, We block their hearing. You can try to guide them but they will never be guided ✦ Your Lord is forgiving, full of Compassion— if He held them to account their torment would be swift. But there is an appointed Day—there is no way to evade it! ✦ We destroyed their cities when they sinned, destroyed them on an appointed Day!

✦

Moses said to his attendant—

"*I am resolved to reach the place where the two seas meet, even if the journey is long*" ✦ When they reached the place, the attendant left behind the fish they'd brought and it wriggled into the sea ✦ A little further on Moses said, "*Let's have our meal—this has been a tiring odyssey!*" ✦ And the lad said, "*Remember when we stopped at the rock? I forgot the fish there and worse yet—the Devil himself made me forget to mention it—*

it wriggled into the sea quite wondrously!" ◆ "That's what we're after!" said Moses so they retraced their steps hastily ◆ And found there one of Our servants, a recipient of Our Clemency and of special Knowledge from Us granted him directly ◆ "May I follow you" Moses asked, "so you can teach me something of the guidance you've been taught?" ◆ And he replied, "You won't be able to forbear my company ◆ How can you forbear when you have no real mastery?" ◆ "I shall God willing forbear," said Moses, "and not disobey you in any way—you shall see" ◆ "If you follow me, unless I myself bring something up," said he, "be sure not to question me" ◆

70

And they set out. They boarded a vessel—and he scuttled it. Moses said, "Won't that cause everyone to drown? You've acted monstrously" ◆ "I told you, didn't I, you won't be able to forbear my company?" ◆ And Moses said, "Do not fault me for my lapse— do not overburden me" ◆

And they set out. They encountered a young man—and he killed him. Moses said, "Have you killed someone for no reason? You've acted terribly!" ◆ "Didn't I tell you that you won't be able to forbear my company?" ◆ "If I question you again" said Moses, "we will part company—you'd be entitled to exact that of me" ◆

And they set out. They reached a town and asked for food but the inhabitants refused all hospitality. They found a wall on the verge of collapse—and he rebuilt it. Moses said "Had you wished you could have asked for a small fee" ◆

"Now you and I part ways" he said — *"But first I shall explain the meaning of the things you were unable to forbear* ✦ *The boat belonged to poor fishermen — I wanted to damage it because a tyrant was close by and seizing every boat forcibly* ✦ *The boy's* ₈₀ *parents were believers we feared he would overburden with his cruelty and blasphemy* ✦ *We wanted their Lord to replace him with someone of greater affection and purity* ✦ *The wall belonged to two orphans in the city: beneath it was buried their rightful treasure. Their father had been virtuous so your Lord wanted them to reach maturity and find their treasure as a mark, a mark of Your Lord's Clemency. I did nothing of my own accord — this is the explanation of what you could not forbear patiently"*

✦

They will ask you about Dhûl-Qarnayn — Reply, *"Let me recount that history"* — ✦

We vested in him earthly authority and access to every passageway ✦ He went along one ✦ Till he reached the sunset and found the Sun setting in a murky pool and a people dwelling not far away. *"Dhul-Qarnayn,"* We said, *"Punish them or treat them amiably!"* ✦ *"I will torment the wicked"* he said, *"And when they return to their Lord He will punish them terribly* ✦ *Those who believe and act virtuously shall have a handsome reward and their tasks will be easy"* ✦

He went along a passageway ✦ Till he reached the sunrise ₉₀ and found the Sun rising upon a people We had not shielded from its intensity ✦ He let them be—what he learned was already encompassed by Our Knowledge and Mastery ✦

He went along a passageway ✦ Till he reached a place between two forbidding ramparts and found a people who understood him with difficulty ✦ *"Dhul-Qarnayn,"* they said, *"Gog and Magog are doing mischief in our land—will you build a barrier between us if we offer to pay?"* ✦ *"Far better,"* he replied, *"Is that authority which my Lord has vested in me—I shall put up a bulwark between you and them if you help with all your might and energy* ✦ *Bring blocks of iron"*—and he filled up the space between the cliffs—*"Now blow the bellows!"*—and there was fire—*"The molten brass to pour on it—now bring that to me!"* ✦ And Gog and Magog were unable to scale it, unable to make the slightest dent ✦ *"This"* he said, *"Is from my Lord's Clemency—my Lord's Promise is always fulfilled—when the Day comes He will level the barrier utterly"* ✦

That Day the multitudes will surge. When the Trumpet sounds
100 We will muster them in Assembly ✦ That Day We will present Hell to the obstinate, to those who could not hear My Reminder, whose eyes were shrouded in obscurity ✦ Do the disbelievers really believe servants of Mine will make better allies than Me? For those who disbelieve We have prepared Hell as a Sanctuary ✦

Declare—*"Shall we tell you who the defeated really are among those who have worked strenuously? ✦ Those who lose themselves in this life thinking they are acting meritoriously* ◆ *who deny their Lord's signs, deny they will meet Him—Their deeds are empty!"*

On the Day of Resurrection, they shall have no standing with Me ◆ Hell—that will be the reward for their blasphemy and for treating Our Signs and Emissaries with mockery ◆ Those who believe and do Good shall have Gardens of Paradise as Sanctuary ◆ Never wishing to leave, remaining there for Eternity◆

Attest—*"If the sea were ink for my Lord's words, it would run dry long before His word ever would"*—even if We were to supply a second sea! ◆

Affirm—*"I am a man like you, one inspired with the Knowledge that* 110 *your God is One. Those who wish to meet their Lord should worship none but Him alone—and act virtuously!"*

(Kahf, 18)

VERSES GLORIFYING GOD

MUSLIMS ARE ENJOINED to glorify and praise God as much as possible, as an acknowledgment that everything exists and happens because of God. The ubiquitous phrase *allâhu akbar*, "God is Supreme," for example, opens the call to prayer (*âdhân*) and is chanted from mosques, in homes, and over the airwaves before each of the five ritual prayers, and the phrase is also pronounced throughout the cycles of the ritual prayers. Together with *subhânallâh*, "God be exalted," and *alhamdu lillâh*, "God be praised," these three expressions of God's glory are known as the Rosary of Fatimah, so called because the Prophet prescribed them to his daughter Fatimah as an easy form of *dhikr* (remembrance). Muslims routinely repeat the Rosary of

Fatimah, especially after the ritual prayers, as well as numerous verses and passages in the Qur'an that glorify and praise God. I include a selection of thirteen of the most frequently invoked ones below.

"BELIEVERS, SEEK HELP"

Believers, seek help through forbearance and prayer—
   God is with those who forbear

(Baqarah 2:153)

"TO GOD WE BELONG"

To God we belong and to God we return

(Baqarah 2:156′)

Your God is One
There is none but He
Ever Compassionate and Full
of Compassion

(Baqarah 2:163)

No compulsion in belief.
What is right is clear from what is wrong.
Whoever renounces false gods and believes in God
grasps the firmest, unbreakable handhold.
God Hears and Sees.

(Baqarah 2:256)

Everything in heaven and on earth
belongs to God.

Whether you reveal what you harbor or conceal it
He will call you all to account.

He decides who deserves forgiveness
He decides who deserves punishment.

God's Power over all
is supreme.

(Baqarah 2:284)

The Emissary believes
in what was revealed to him from his Lord:
likewise the believers.

All believe in God, His Angels,
His Books and Emissaries.
They say, "We make no distinction between any
of His Emissaries."
"We hear, and obey,
and seek Your forgiveness, Lord.
You are the journey's end."

God burdens no soul beyond its capacity.
It earns with its deeds
and bears its misdeeds.

"Take us not to task
if we forget or transgress.
Lord, do not place a burden on us,
as you did on those who came before us.
Do not burden us with more
than we have strength to bear.

Pardon us,
forgive us,
have mercy on us.
You are our Guide.

And help us prevail over
those who have no faith.

(Baqarah 2:285–86)

Declare—

God,
Your rule is absolute.

You bestow rule
on those You choose,
You divest rule
from those You choose.

You exalt those You choose,
You abase those You choose.

The Good lies in your hands.
Your power over all reigns supreme.

◆

You merge the night into day,
You merge the day into night.

From the dead you produce the living,
From the living you produce the dead.

And You provide
to those You choose
without measure.

(Âl ʿImrân 3:26–27)

We need
only God—
The very best protector

(Âl 'Imrân 3:173')

"THERE IS NO GOD BUT YOU—EXALTED!"

There is no God but You—Exalted!
Truly have I acted grievously!

(Anbiyâ' 21:87')

"GOD ON HIGH REIGNS IN TRUTH!"

God on High reigns in Truth!
There is no God but He—
Lord of the Magnificent Throne.

(Mu'minûn 23:116)

God is
The Light of Heaven and Earth

Imagine His Light as a niche—
within it a lamp encased in glass
like a gleaming star
a lamp kindled
from a hallowed olive tree found
neither in east nor west
its oil untouched by fire
almost aglow

Light upon Light!

God guides whom He wishes to the Light
and through examples explains
for all to understand

Nothing is beyond His ken

(Nûr 24:35, "Âyat al-Nûr")

May Your Lord,
the Lord of Power,
be exalted far above
what they can describe.

May peace descend
on all His heralds.

All Praise
to God,
Lord of all Worlds.

(Sâffât 37:180–82)

He is God,
There is no god but He

Knower of the Seen and Unseen

Ever Compassionate
and Full of Compassion

He is God
There is no god but He

Sovereign
Holy
Serene

Protecting
and True

Exalted
Commanding
Magnificent

Exalted far above
what they can portray

He is God
Creator
Maker
Originator

The divine epithets beautifully express
Him

All that lies in Heaven and Earth
Sings his glory

He is Almighty
Wise

(Hashr 59:22–24)

SUPPLICATION VERSES

THE COLLECTION OF FORTY-THREE Qur'anic supplications that begin with the phrase *rab'banâ*, literally "Our Lord," and *rab'bî*, literally "My Lord," are referred to as The Forty *Rab'banâ*. As might be expected, all of them are uttered by individuals entreating God—Adam after the expulsion from the Garden, Abraham when he erects the Kaaba, believers seeking God's mercy and grace, and so on. The Forty *Rab'banâ* form part of many devotional practices. Some Muslims memorize all of them. In the daily prayer book, *al-Hizb al-A'zam*, they form part of the recitational practice (*wazîfah*) for Saturday. I include below ten of the most commonly invoked ones.

"Accept this from us, Lord,
You who Hear and Know."

(Baqarah 2:127′)

"Lord, give us good in this world,
and good in the next

And protect us
from the fire's torment."

(Baqarah 2:201')

"LORD, DO NOT LET OUR HEARTS STRAY"

"Lord, do not let our hearts stray
once you have set us aright—
Bestow Your Mercy on us
Without end!"

(Âl ʿImrân 3:8)

"Lord, we heard a call
calling us to faith —

'Believe in your Lord!'
it said, and we did.

Lord, forgive us our transgressions,
absolve us of the wrongs we've done

And when You take us,
count us among the virtuous!"

(Âl 'Imrân 3:193)

"Lord, we have wronged ourselves—
If You are not forgiving and merciful toward us
We will be lost!"

(A'râf 7:23')

"My Lord, make me constant in Prayer,
along with my descendants.
Accept my supplication.

Lord, when the Day of Reckoning comes
forgive me, my parents, and all who believe."

(Ibrâhîm 14:40–41)

"MY LORD, SHOW THEM MERCY"

"My Lord, show them mercy,
just as they did when they raised me."

(Isrâ' 17:24')

"Lord, grant us spouses and children
who will be the light of our eyes

And make of us paragons
for the reverent."

(Furqân 25:74')

"Forgive us, Lord,
and our brethren who preceded us as believers
and do not let us harbor rancor for any believers—
You are full of Kindness and Compassion."

(Hashr 59:10′)

"IN YOU, WE PLACE OUR TRUST, LORD"

"In You, we place our trust, Lord,
and to You alone we turn—
You are our journey's end."

(Mumtahanah 60:4')

sadaqallâhul 'azîm

I describe below a handful of popular *wazîfahs*, or recommended rec-
itation practices, to give an idea of the commonality of Qur'anic
surahs and passages read and recited devotionally around the world; I
mark with asterisks the surahs or passages I translate in this volume.

◆

In *The Book of Assistance*, a guide for spiritual purification in wide
use especially in Yemen, West Africa, and Southeast Asia, and, once
translated into English, increasingly in the United Kingdom and North
America, the seventeenth-century Sufi master Imâm Haddâd enjoins
the reading of the following "seven saving surahs" every night:

> Surah Sajdah (32)
> * Surah Yâ Sîn (36)
> Surah Dukhân (44)
> * Surah Wâqiʿah (56)
> Surah Hashr (59)
> * Surah Mulk (67)
> * Surah Insân (76)

> (Imâm ʿAbd Allâh ibn ʿAlawî al-Haddâd, *The Book of Assistance*,
> trans. Mostafa Badawi [Lexington, KY: Fons Vitae, 2010].)

◆

Imâm Haddâd also compiled *The Haddâd Breviary*, also used around
the world—my copy is from Sri Lanka. It comprises a series of pas-
sages from the Qur'an, followed by supplications, and invocations,

intended to be recited in one sitting. The Qur'anic material consists of:

* Surah Fâtihah (1)
* Âyat al-Kursî (Baqarah 2:255)
* Baqarah 2:285–86
* Surah Ikhlâs (112)
* Surah Falaq (113)
* Surah Nâs (114)

('Abd Allah al-Haddâd, *Rathib Al Haddad,*
trans. Yusuf Ahamed [Colombo: Economic Times, 1991].)

◆

When I returned from Mecca in 1994, I brought home a pocket-sized booklet that lacked publication information but seemed to be available everywhere. I found the same booklet there in 2022. It comprises the following six surahs:

* Surah Kahf (18)
  Surah Dukhân (44)
* Surah Wâqi'ah (56)
* Surah Yâ Sîn (36)
* Surah Rahmân (55)
* Surah Mulk (67)

◆

One of the most popular South Asian Muslim wazîfahs is the *Manzil,* or *Lectionary.* It consists in reading the following:

* Surah Fâtihah (1)
Surah Baqarah
   * 2:1–5
   * 2:163
   2:255–57 (* 255–56)
   * 2:284–86
Âl 'Imrân
   3:18
   * 3:26–27
A'râf 7:54–56
Isrâ' 17:110–11
Mu'minûn 23:115–18 (*116)
Sâffât 37:1–11
* Rahmân 55:33–40
Hashr 59:21–24 (*22–24)
Jinn 72:1–4
* Surah Kâfirûn (109)
* Surah Ikhlâs (112)
* Surah Falaq (113)
* Surah Nâs (114)

> (*Chôbîs sûratên ma'a manzil va-maqbûl du'â'ên*
> [Delhi: Idara Isha'at-e-Diniyat, n.d.].)

◆

In another popular South Asian collection, the following Quranic recitations are recommended:

* Surah Yâ Sîn (36)
Surah Sajdah (32)

* Surah Wâq'iah (56)
* Surah Mulk (67)
  The *Manzil* [see above]
* The Forty *Rab'banâ* [10 are included here]
* Âyat al-Kursî (Baqarah 2:255)
* Surah Qadr (97)
* Surah Zalzalah (99)
* Surah 'Âdiyât (100)
* Surah Takâthur (102)
* Surah Nasr (110)
* Surah Kâfirûn (109)
* Surah Kahf (18)
  Surah Dukhân (44)

(*Duas for Contentment of the Heart*
[Majmu'a Wazaif] [New Delhi: Idara, 2006].)

◆

The following is from a South African daily prayer book, one my wife uses every day:

* Surah Kahf (18)
  Surah Sajdah (32)
* Surah Yâ Sîn (36)
  Surah Fussilat (41)
  Surah Shûrâ (42)
  Surah Dukhân (44)
  Surah Muhammad (47)
  Surah Fath (48)
* Surah Rahmân (55)

* Surah Wâqi'ah (56)
  Surah Mujâdilah (58)
  Surah Jumu'ah (62)
  Surah Taghâbun (64)
  Surah Talâq (65)
  Surah Tahrîm (66)
* Surah Mulk (67)
  Surah Qalam (68)
  Surah Ma'ârij (70)
  Surah Muzzammil (73)
  Surah Muddaththir (74)
* Surah Qadr (97)
  Surah Fajr (89)
  Âl 'Imrân 3:190–200 (*193)
* Baqarah 2:284–86
  Hashr 59:18–24 (*22–24)
* Surah Ikhlâs (112)
* Surah Falaq (113)
* Surah Nâs (114)
* Surah Kâfirûn (109)
* Surah Fâtihah (1)
* Âyat al-Kursî—Baqarah 2:255

(*Selected Suras and Prayers* [Durban: Impress, n.d.].)

◆

The following list is not from a *wazîfah* but is a selection made by the Royal Aal al-Bayt Institute for Islamic Thought, based in Amman, Jordan, for a commissioned translation of selections from a multivolume commentary of the Qur'an by the ninth-to-tenth-century scholar al-

Tabarî. The Foundation sought to identify surahs and passages "associated with special blessings or qualities."

       * Surah Fâtihah (1)
       Baqarah
            * 2:255
            * 2:284–86
       Âl 'Imrân
           3:7
           3:18
       Tawbah 9:128–29
       * Kahf 18:60–82
       Surah Sajdah (32)
       * Surah Yâ Sîn (36)
       Zumar 39:53–55
       Surah Dukhân (44)
       * Surah Rahmân (55)
       * Surah Wâqi'ah (56)
       Surah Hadîd (57)
       Hashr 59:18–24 (*22–24)
       * Surah Mulk (67)
       Surah Qiyâmah (75)
       * Surah A'lâ (87)
       Surah Shams (91)
       Surah Layl (92)
       * Surah Zalzalah (99)
       * Surah 'Âdiyât (100)
       * Surah Takâthur (102)
       * Surah Kâfirûn (109)

* Surah Nasr (110)
* Surah Ikhlâs (112)
* Surah Falaq (113)
* Surah Nâs (114)

(Tabarî, *Selections from "The Comprehensive Exposition of the Interpretation of the Verses of the Qur'ân,"* 2 vol., trans. Scott C. Lucas [Cambridge: Royal Aal Al-Bayt Institute and Islamic Texts Society, 2017].)

Allâh	the Arabic word for God.
âyah, pl. *âyât*	Qur'anic verse(s).
Âyat al-Kursî	the Throne Verse (Baqarah 2:255).
Âyat al-Nûr	the Verse of Light (Nûr 24:35).
basmalah	the phrase *bismillâhir rahmânir rahîm,* "In the name of God, full of Compassion and ever Compassionate," which precedes every surah (except Surah Tawbah, 9) and which is recited before undertaking any task.
dhikr	measured repetition of Qur'an or pious expressions of praise in remembrance of God as a recollection of God's omnipresence and majesty.
du'â	supplication and petition to God; well wishes expressed as prayers for oneself and for others.
Eid	shorthand for Eid al-Fitr, the high holiday following the end of Ramadan, a time of rejoicing, and for Eid al-Adha, the high holiday during the pilgrimage season; there are congregational prayers on the mornings of both Eids with accompanying sermons (*khutbah*).
hadith	a saying or reported action attributed to the Prophet Muhammad.
Hadith	the corpus of hadiths.
hâfiz	a person who has memorized the Qur'an in its entirety.
hizb	the term for the division of the Qur'an into sixtieths, to guide completion of a reading of the entire Qur'an (*khatm*) in two months.
imam	any leader of congregational prayer.

Imam	the title given by Shiites to the prime spiritual leader.
Jibrîl	the Archangel Gabriel, the angel of revelation in Islam.
jinn	an order of creation, created from fire; like humans, they inhabit the earth and like humans can choose to believe or disbelieve. There is a surah named for them (Jinn, 72) and at least one (Rahmân, 55) also addressed to them. Iblîs (Satan) is held to be a jinn.
Jumu ʿah	lit. gathering; the shorthand name for both Friday (*yawm al-Jumu ʿah*) and for the Friday prayer (*salât al-Jumu ʿah*), both also commonly called Jummah.
juz ʾ	the term for the division of the Qur ʾan into thirtieths, to guide completion of a reading of the entire Qur ʾan (*khatm*) in one month.
khatîb	the sermon-giver, at the Friday congregational prayer (*Jumu ʿah*) and at the two Eid prayers.
khatm	one complete reading or recitation of the entire Qur ʾan.
khutbah	the sermon on Friday or on the two Eids.
laylat al-qadr	the Night of Awe, a night in the month of Ramadan on which the Qur ʾan is said to have first been revealed from on high.
manzil	the term for the division of the Qur ʾan into sevenths, to guide completion of a *khatm* in one week.
Manzil	a popular and influential selection of *âyah*s and surahs widely circulated in South Asia and in the South Asian diaspora.
Mecca	(Makkah in Arabic) the birthplace of Muhammad and in pre-Islamic times a trading city and pilgrimage destination. It is Islam's holiest city and the destination of the *hajj* and *ʿumrah*, the annual

and year-round Muslim pilgrimages, respectively. Muslims face Mecca when performing ritual prayers.

Medina (Madînah in Arabic), literally "city," from *Madînat al-Nabî*, the City of the Prophet, who emigrated there in 610 and remained until his death in 632.

minbar a raised pulpit in a mosque, usually consisting of three or seven steps.

mu'awwidhatân "the two protecting surahs," a name given to Surahs Falaq (113) and Nâs (114), so called because reciting them provides protection from all manner of harm.

Muhammad prophet of Islam, born in 570 in the city of Mecca, in western Arabia.

mus'haf a bound or printed copy of the Qur'an.

Qur'an the revealed Word of God, as transmitted by the Archangel Gabriel to Muhammad.

rab'banâ the name given to the supplication passages in the Qur'an that open with the phrase *rab'banâ*, literally "Our Lord," or *rab'bî*, literally "My Lord."

rak'ah the cycle of the ritual prayer. The five obligatory daily prayers have a fixed number of cycles:

fajr (predawn)	2 *rak'ahs*
zuhr (postzenith)	4 *rak'ahs*
'asr (mid- to late afternoon)	4 *rak'ahs*
maghrib (postsunset)	3 *rak'ahs*
'ishâ' (nighttime)	4 *rak'ahs*

Ramadan the ninth month of the Islamic lunar calendar, during which fasting is prescribed, on one night of which, *laylat al-qadr*, the Qur'an is said to have first been revealed from on high.

rûh	literally "soul" or "Spirit."
rukû'	the paragraphs into which the Qur'anic text is divided; also the name of the bowing motion in the ritual prayer.
saj'	Arabic rhyming cadenced prose, a feature of 85 percent of the Qur'an.
salât, salâh	the ritual prayer or prayer rite; five specific ones are prescribed daily (see *rak'ah* above), and many more are performed in emulation of the Prophet at specific times (for example, on Friday, on the two Eids, at funerals, when first entering a mosque to give thanks, as acts of devotion, and so on).
sîrah	literally "biography"; account of the life of the Prophet Muhammad.
Sufi	loosely "mystic"; originally an ascetic who renounced worldly matters, later applied to any individual who adopted certain practices of mystical piety (notably *dhikr*).
surah	a Qur'anic "chapter."
tarâwîh	the ritual prayers performed (by Sunnis) every night in Ramadan, ideally in congregation.
verse	literally "sign"; common English term for *âyah, âyat* (pl. *âyât*), the verse divisions of the Qur'an's surahs.
wazîfah	a set of recitations, of passages from the Qur'an or of supplications, as prescribed by pious figures or Sufis; also the term for the printed record of such prescriptions.

Invocation

The invocation *a'ûdhu billâhi min ash-shaytânir rajîm*, "I seek refuge with God from the accursed Satan," is pronounced one time before beginning any recitation from the Qur'an.

It is followed by the *basmalah*, the phrase *bismillâhir rahmânir rahîm*, "In the name of God, ever Compassionate and full of Compassion," which is recited at the beginning of every surah but one (Surah Tawbah, 9, Repentance) and before reciting or quoting any passage from the Qur'an. It is also uttered in full, or in its shortened form, *bismillâh*, when undertaking any task whatsoever.

Epigraph

Alif Lâm Mîm: the names of three of the twenty-eight letters of the Arabic alphabet. Altogether fourteen different letters appear alone or in various combinations at the beginning of twenty-nine surahs. Called *fawâtih al-suwar*, "surah openers," or *al-muqatta'ât*, "the discrete letters," their precise meaning eludes scholars, hence the common English designation "the mysterious letters." These letters and letter combinations figure prominently in Sufi devotional materials.

the pious and the reverent: using a doublet to render *al-muttaqîn*, often translated as "God-fearing" and "God-conscious."

THE FÂTIHAH

The Opening Prayer

In the Name of God / Ever Compassionate and Full of Compassion: in the case of the Fâtihah alone, the *basmalah* has come to be regarded by many as the surah's opening verse.

You Alone we beseech: inverting this with "And to You Alone we pray."

those who please You: literally "Those with whom You are pleased."

Amen: although it does not form part of the Qur'anic text, the response *Âmîn* is always uttered, audibly or inaudibly, after recitation of the Fâtihah. It is also uttered after expressions of wish, benediction, and prayer.

THE SHORT SURAHS

Morning Light

there has been no slight: literally "He is not displeased."

unaware: more literally "lost," "unguided."

Solace

Didn't I: opting here for the more personal first person singular rather than the royal *We,* in keeping with the intimate tone of the surah.

This shall pass. / This too shall pass: literally "For indeed with difficulty (comes) ease / indeed with difficulty (comes) ease," a reassurance that things will get better.

The Fig

city of sanctuary: literally "secure city," namely Mecca, specifically the precincts of the Kaaba, which was, even before the advent of Islam, a sanctuary where no weapons or shedding of blood was permitted.

The Clot

Proclaim: iqra ', usually translated "Recite" or "Read." I opt for a verb that presages the Prophet's ministry.

Angels of Havoc: al-zabâniyah, taken by most Qur'an commentators and translators to mean myrmidons, guardian angels of Hell.

Bow down: literally "prostrate." This is one of the fourteen Qur'anic verses (or fifteen, by another reckoning) that mention prostration. Readers or reciters pause and prostrate when they reach these verses.

Awe

the Night of Awe: laylat al-qadr, typically translated "Night of Power," "Night of Destiny," and less often "Night of Glory" and "Night of Decree."

What, you ask, is . . . ?: the rhetorical query *mâ adrâka mâ*, literally "what will inform you what is?" which I translate differently in different places based on context. In Surah Qâri'ah (101), I render it "What precisely is?" and in Surah Humazah (104) "How will you know?"

a thousand months or more: literally "a thousand months." I add "or more" to convey the fact that the use of a thousand here—and in Arabic generally—does not denote an exact figure but implies a very large number.

Spirit: al-rûh, understood by most Qur'an commentators to be a reference to Jibrîl, the Archangel Gabriel.

Clear Evidence

true affirmations: kutubun qayyimah, rendered in a wide variety of ways by translators, including "canonical writings," "testament," "true scriptures," "upright precepts."

devotion . . . faith: dîn, a word that has come to mean "religion," "creed," or, as I render it in Surah Kâfirûn (109), "way."

rivers gently flowing: literally "rivers flowing underfoot."

Convulsion

the Almighty shall make the earth reveal/what He has in store: literally "the earth shall tell all its stories as inspired by your Lord."

Coursers

coursing chargers: galloping horses.

The Shattering

The Shattering: al-qâri'ah, one of numerous terms in the Qur'an used to describe clamorous and especially cataclysmic aspects of the end of the world and Judgment Day.

will head to the Abyss: literally "his matrix/mother will be the bottomless pit."

Vying

about your revelries: literally about "the blessing" or "the pleasure," understood in two very different ways by Qur'an commentators and translators, either as God's blessing and favor, or as worldly pleasure, which I adopt here.

Declining Day

declining day: 'asr, sometimes rendered "epoch," but much likelier an invocation of part of the day, as is the case in most other Qur'anic oaths.

tenacity: sabr, a fundamental concept in the Qur'an, encompassing the meanings of holding fast, showing fortitude, forbearing, accepting God's will, especially in the face of adversity, and having patience.

Slander

who slander and defame: literally "every scandalmonger and backbiter."

The War Elephant

Ponder: literally "Have you not seen how . . . ?," a recurring phrase in the Qur'an, asking the reader and listener to consider signs of God's power and decree.

the people on elephant back: according to Qur'an commentators, a reference to the unsuccessful attack on Mecca by Abrahah, an Abyssinian general who ruled Yemen, in the year of the Prophet Muhammad's birth, traditionally reckoned as the year 570.

The Quraysh

Quraysh: the Prophet Muhammad's tribe.

Shrine: literally "House" or "Temple"; here the Kaaba is meant. The Quraysh were custodians of the shrine and its precincts.

Simple Kindness

simple kindness and the smallest deed: expanding *al-mâ'ûn,* literally "basic assistance," to convey both the demeanor and the aid itself.

Abundance

I lavished . . . : as in Surah Inshirâh (Solace, 94), opting here for the first person singular over the royal We, to retain the intimate tone.

A heavenly spring: kawthar, a figurative description that has also been taken literally as the name of a river, spring, or pool in heaven.

Disbelievers

Answer: qul, literally "Say," a common rhetorical expression that prefaces many supplicatory passages. I translate it differently in different places.

Palm Fiber

Abû Lahab: literally "The possessor of the flame," the nickname of one of the uncles of the Prophet Muhammad who was a leader of the Qurasyh and a fierce opponent of his nephew's teachings. The moniker may be a reference to his ruddy complexion or red hair. The "flaming fire" of verse 3 is a play on this.

his power will shrivel: literally "his hands will shrivel," an expression describing destruction.

his woman: likely a reference to Umm Jamîl, who, like her husband, was bitterly opposed to the Prophet Muhammad and was said to strew twisted bundles of palm fiber along his path in order to cause him injury.

Sincere Belief

Flawless: samad, a characterization of God, the many interpretations and consequently renderings of which include "absolute," "constantly sought," "eternal," "everlasting refuge," "rock," and "self-sufficient."

Daybreak

spitting on knots: a way to cast a spell on someone, as two women are reported to have done to the Prophet Muhammad, occasioning the revelation of this surah.

Humanity

the Whisperer's calumny: literally the "slinking" or "recoiling" or "retreating" whisperer.

ÂYAT AL-KURSÎ

The Throne Verse

He, without beginning or end: literally "the Living, the Self-Subsisting." I favor nonanimate characterization here.

Unwearying, untouched by Time: literally "Neither age nor sleep overtake him."

SURAH YÂ SÎN

Yâ Sîn

Yâ Sîn: a "surah opener" (see Alif Lâm Mîm note). This particular combination occurs only at the beginning of this surah. (Yâ Sîn is also one of the many names for the Prophet Muhammad.)

this discerning Recitation: rendered by many translators as "the Wise Qur'an" or "the Qur'an, full of Wisdom."

the city—messengers were sent to its populace: the city is held by many Qur'an commentators to be Antioch, and the messengers to be emissaries sent by Jesus.

Enter Paradise: the man is stoned by his people and is admitted to Paradise when he dies.

Blast: the Blast of the Trumpet announcing the end of the world and Judgment Day. According to tradition the trumpet will be blown by the Archangel Isrâfîl (Raphael).

Disgraceful Humanity!: literally "Alas for Humanity" or "Woe to the believers."

We have not taught him poetry and verse — that is below his status: the Prophet Muhammad is meant; this is a rebuttal of the accusation that he was a mere poet and the Qur'an mere poetry of his creation.

Reminder: one of several ways the Qur'an (literally the "Recitation") characterizes itself. Some translators render this word, *dhikr,* as "Message," "Remembrance," or "Revelation."

as He decrees: I have added this phrase as it is strongly implied by the widely cited immediately preceding verse.

SURAHS FOR DAILY AND WEEKLY RECITATION

The Great News

Lamp: the Sun.

The Inevitable

Oh, and *Woe* two lines later: opting to use different words to render the Arabic *mâ,* to capture the very different tenor of each use.

ambrosia's decanter: opting to describe both the contents and the vessel, rendered variously by translators, including "goblets, beakers," "glasses and flagons," and "chalices and pitchers."

blessed . . . wretched: as with "Oh" and "Woe" above, opting to use different words still to render *mâ* here.

Zaqqûm: a tree in Hell, the fruit of which is described at Dukhân 44:45 as being like molten metal.

The Kingdom

Kingdom: rendered by other translators as "Authority," "Dominion," and "Sovereignty."

lightbursts: literally "lamps" or "lights."

The Ever Compassionate

proportion: opting for "proportion" to render *mîzân*, "balance."

which then of your Lord's wonders do you both deny in vain?: this surah's celebrated refrain, repeated thirty-one times in the space of sixty-five verses, making it the most repeated refrain in any surah. The two addressees meant by "you both" are jinn and humans, as confirmed in verse 33.

wonders: I opt for "wonders" for *âlâ*', a word that conveys the wondrous nature of what is described as opposed to the more common renderings, "blessings," "bounties" or "favors."

both risings and both settings: "risings" and "settings" are in the dual in the Arabic and sometimes rendered "the two easts" and "the two wests."

Humankind

Salsabîl: a fountain or a spring in Paradise.

gradually: *tanzîlâ*, understood by some Qur'an commentators and translators to mean "in truth" or "as a revelation" but more commonly taken to mean that the Qur'an was revealed in portions (as little as an *âyah* or as much as a whole surah) over the course of the Prophet Muhammad's twenty-three years of prophethood.

FRIDAY VERSES AND SURAHS

"Call on Me—I will answer"

Call on Me—I will answer: this passage echoes the fuller Baqarah 2:186: "My worshipers ask you about Me: I am near, and I respond to any who call on Me. So let them respond to My call and believe in Me, that they may be rightly guided."

The Most High

in Abraham's Scrolls, and Moses' Scripture: the Qur'an also mentions in other passages the scriptures of David, Jesus, and Muhammad.

The Enfoldment

loftily displayed . . . carefully conveyed . . . plentifully arrayed . . . beautifully laid: adding the adverbs, whose meanings are implied here, for rhetorical effect.

The Cave

Companions of the Cave: widely understood to be a reference to the Seven Sleepers, youths who in the third century hid inside a cave in Ephesus to escape persecution for their Christian beliefs and who emerged some three hundred years later.

Tablet: al-raqîm, also interpreted by some Qur'an commentators as variously referring to an inscription, to the name of the Companions' dog (mentioned in verse 18), and to the place or mountain where the cave was situated.

if God wills: the Qur'anic passage that charges believers to say "inshallah" when speaking of a future event, of a possible occurrence, or of an intention.

Iblîs: the given name of the jinn (that is, not a fallen angel) who defied God by refusing to bow to Adam. The Qur'an also calls him Shaytân (Satan).

Emissary: the Qur'an refers to those whom God has inspired with a message or revealed a scripture as *mursal* (emissary), *rasûl* (messenger), and *nabî* (prophet). I use emissary for all three.

hastily: adding this adverb, implicit in the action of Moses turning back to find the object of his quest.

one of Our servants: though unnamed, he is identified in a hadith as al-Khidr, a long-liver, that is, someone who lives for centuries. He is said to have tutored countless prophets and to have met the Prophet Muhammad.

Dhûl-Qarnayn: literally "the two-horned," a figure possibly to be connected to Alexander the Great.

Gog and Magog: legendary figures or peoples believed to be held back by the barrier built by Alexander the Great.

the Trumpet: the Trumpet blown by the Archangel Israfil (Raphael), announcing the end of the world and Judgment Day.

Declare: qul, literally "Say," appearing three times in quick succession, and which, as elsewhere, I translate differently (here subsequently "Attest," then "Affirm").

VERSES GLORIFYING GOD

"To God we belong"

To God we belong and to God we return: also uttered upon learning of someone's passing.

"The Emissary believes"

The Emissary believes . . . who have no faith: held to be the only two verses in the Qur'an that the Archangel Gabriel was hearing for the first time when he conveyed them to the Prophet Muhammad.

"Declare—God, your rule is absolute"

rule: opting for "rule" here over "Kingdom."

"We need only God"

We need only God—The very best protector: a statement attributed to the members of the early Muslim community when they were told they would be facing a great army.

"There is no God but You—Exalted!"

There is no God but You—Exalted! . . . : the words uttered by Jonah when he was in despair.

"He is God, There is no god but He"

The divine epithets beautifully express Him: literally "To Him belong the beautiful names."

SUPPLICATION VERSES

"Accept this from us, Lord"

"Accept this from us, Lord . . .": uttered by Abraham and Ishmael after they built the Kaaba in Mecca (an event described at Âl 'Imrân 3:96).

"Lord, give us good in this world"

"Lord, give us good in this world . . .": an example of what righteous people pray for. The Prophet Muhammad is reported to have said that this one supplication alone suffices for the believer.

"Lord, do not let our hearts stray"

"Lord, do not let our hearts stray . . .": a supplication attributed to believers endowed with understanding who accept the revelation of the Qur'an.

"Lord, we heard a call"

"Lord, we heard a call . . .": a supplication attributed to believers who contemplate creation and continually praise God.

"Lord, we have wronged ourselves"

"Lord, we have wronged ourselves . . .": uttered by Adam and Eve after they disobeyed God's command not to approach the tree.

"My Lord, make me constant in Prayer"

"My Lord, make me constant in Prayer . . .": the last of a sequence of supplications uttered by Abraham.

"My Lord, show them mercy"

"My Lord, show them mercy . . .": a supplication enjoined on the Prophet Muhammad and by extension on all believers. It is preceded by a verse in which believers are told not to become exasperated with their parents when they are elderly.

"Lord, grant us spouses and children who will be the light of our eyes"

"Lord, grant us . . .": A supplication attributed to exemplary believers—humble, gentle, just, measured, and upright—who will as a result be rewarded with the highest place in heaven.

"Forgive us, Lord, and our brethren"

"Forgive us, Lord, and our brethren . . .": possibly spoken by those Meccans who subsequently emigrated to Medina, and more generally by all who subsequently embraced the faith.

"In You, we place our trust, Lord"

"In You, we place our trust, Lord . . .": uttered by Abraham to God, upon realizing that his father will remain an unbeliever.

Valediction

sadaqallâhul ʿazîm: "Almighty God's Word is True," uttered after reading, reciting, or hearing Qurʾanic passages recited (outside of the ritual prayer).

FURTHER READING

I favor the following full translations of the Qur'an:

> Abdel Haleem, M. A. S., trans. *The Qur'an: A New Translation.* Corrected ed. Oxford: Oxford University Press, 2008.
>
> Khalidi, Tarif, trans. *The Qur'an: A New Translation.* London: Penguin, 2008.
>
> Khan, Waheeduddin, and Farida Khanam, trans. *The Quran.* Delhi: Goodword, 2014.

For readers wishing to learn more about the Qur'an and Islam, I recommend the following selected books, organized by subject matter, as useful starting points; I include some older works which I believe continue to be useful.

I mark with an asterisk those works I regard as especially accessible for readers encountering these subjects for the first time.

Introductions and Reading Guides to the Qur'an and Islam

> * Ali, Kecia, and Oliver Leaman. *Islam: The Key Concepts.* London: Routledge, 2008.
>
> * Allen, Roger, and Shawkat M. Toorawa, eds. *Islam: A Short Guide to the Faith.* Grand Rapids, MI: William B. Eerdmans, 2011.
>
> * Daftary, Farhad, and Zulfikar Hirji. *Islam: An Illustrated Journey.* London: Azimuth, 2018.
>
> Denny, Fredrick. *Introduction to Islam,* 4th new ed. New York: Routledge, 2017.
>
> * Elias, Jamal. *Islam.* London: Routledge, 1999.
>
> * Ernst, Carl W. *How to Read the Qur'an: A New Guide, with Select Translations.* Edinburgh: Edinburgh University Press, 2012.

Esack, Fareed. *The Qur'an: A Beginner's Guide.* Oxford: Oneworld, 2009.

* Gade, Anna M. *The Qur'an: An Introduction.* Oxford: Oneworld, 2016.

* Lawrence, Bruce B. *The Koran in English: A Biography.* Princeton: Princeton University Press, 2017.

* Mattson, Ingrid. *The Story of the Qur'an: Its History and Place in Muslim Life.* 2nd ed. Chichester, West Sussex: Wiley-Blackwell, 2013.

McAuliffe, Jane, ed. *The Qur'ān: A Norton Critical Edition.* New York: W. W. Norton, 2017. Includes a full translation revising Mohammed Marmaduke Pickthall.

Mir, Mustansir. *Understanding the Islamic Scripture: A Study of Selected Passages from the Qur'an.* London: Routledge, 2017.

* Omaar, Rageh, et al. *The Islam Book: Big Ideas Simply Explained.* London: Dorling Kindersley, 2020.

* Renard, John. *Seven Doors to Islam: Spirituality and the Religious Life of Muslims.* Berkeley: University of California Press, 1996.

Robinson, Neal. *Discovering the Qur'an: A Contemporary Approach to a Veiled Text.* 2nd ed. Washington, DC: Georgetown University Press, 2004.

Sardar, Ziauddin. *Reading the Qur'an: The Contemporary Relevance of the Sacred Text of Islam.* Oxford: Oxford University Press, 2017.

* Siddiqui, Mona. *How to Read the Qur'an.* London: Granta, 2014.

Sinai, Nicolai. *The Qur'an: A Historical-Critical Introduction.* Edinburgh: Edinburgh University Press, 2017.

Von Denffer, Ahmad. *'Ulûm al-Qur'ân: An Introduction to the Sciences of the Qur'ân.* Rev. ed. Markfield, Leicestershire: Islamic Foundation, 1994.

Watt, William Montgomery, and Richard Bell. *Introduction to the Qur'an.* Rev. and enlarged ed. Edinburgh: Edinburgh University Press, 1977.

Manuals and Prayer Books of Muslim Devotion

Duas for The Contentment of the Heart: Majmu'a Wazaif. New Delhi: Millat Book Centre, n.d.

Al-Ghazâlî, Abû Hâmid. *Invocations and Supplications: Kitâb al-adhkâr wa'l-da'awât. Book IX of The Revival of the Religious Sciences: Ihyâ' 'ulûm al-dîn.* 4th ed., trans. Kojiro Nakamura. Cambridge: Islamic Texts Society, 2010.

Al-Haddad, Imam Abdallah Ibn 'Alawi. *The Book of Assistance.* Trans. Mostafa Badawi. Lexington, KY: Fons Vitae, 2010.

The Great Prayer Book of Islam (Al-Hizbul-A'zam) with English Translation and Introductory Comments. Karachi: Taj Company, n.d.

Ibn al-Jazarî, Ahmad. *Al Hisn Al Haseen.* Karachi: Darul Ishaat, 2008.

Siddiqui, M. 'Abdul Hamid, trans. *Prayers of the Prophet (Masnun Du'â'ên).* Karachi: Sh. Muhammad Ashraf, 1987.

Classical Qur'an Commentary, Studies of Muslim Devotion, and Studies of the Qur'an

Abu Zayd, Nasr Hamid. *Critique of Religious Discourse.* Trans. Jonathan Wright. New Haven: Yale University Press, 2018.

Ayoub, Mahmoud. *The Qur'an and Its Interpreters.* Vols. 1 and 2. Albany: State University of New York Press, 1984, 1992.

Cornell, Vincent, and Bruce Lawrence, eds. *The Wiley-Blackwell Companion to Islamic Spirituality.* Hoboken, NJ: John Wiley and Sons, 2023.

Déroche, François. *The One and the Many: The Early History of the Qur'an.* Trans. Malcolm DeBevoise. New Haven: Yale University Press, 2021.

Gätje, Helmut. *The Qur'an and Its Exegesis: Selected Texts with Classical and Modern Muslim Interpretations.* Trans. Alford T. Welch. Oxford: Oneworld, 2008.

Haleem, Muhammad Abdel. *Understanding the Qur'an: Themes and Styles.* London: I. B. Tauris, 2011.

Ibrahim, Celene. *Women and Gender in the Qur'an.* Oxford University Press, 2020.

Katz, Marion. *Prayer in Islamic Thought and Practice.* Cambridge: Cambridge University Press, 2013.

Kermani, Navid. *God Is Beautiful: The Aesthetic Experience of the Quran.* Trans. Tony Crawford. Cambridge: Polity, 2015.

al-Mahallî, Jalâl al-dîn and Jalâl al-dîn al-Suyûtî. *Tafsîr al-Jalâlayn.* Trans. Feras Hamza. Lexington, KY: Fons Vitae, 2008. Includes a full translation.

Nasr, Seyyed Hossein, Caner Dagli, Maria Massi Dakake, Joseph B. Lumbard, and Mohammed Rustom, eds. and trans. *The Study Quran.* New York: HarperOne, 2015. Includes a full translation.

Nelson, Kristina. *The Art of Reciting the Qur'an,* 2nd ed. Austin: University of Texas Press, 2015.

Neuwirth, Angelika. *The Qur'an and Late Antiquity: A Shared Heritage.* Trans. Samuel Wilder. Oxford: Oxford University Press, 2019.

Padwick, Constance. *Muslim Devotions: A Study of Prayer-manuals in Common Use.* 1961; Oxford: Oneworld, 1996.

Rahman, Fazlur. *Major Themes of the Qur'an.* 2nd ed. Chicago: University of Chicago Press, 2009.

Renard, John. *Windows on the House of Islam: Muslim Sources on Spirituality and Religious Life.* Berkeley: University of California Press, 1998.

Tabarî, Muhammad ibn Jarîr. *Selections from "The Comprehensive Exposition of the Interpretation of the Verses of the Qur'an."* Trans. Scott C. Lucas. Cambridge: Islamic Texts Society, 2017.

Further Translations of the Qur'an

Listed chronologically.

Yusuf Ali, Abdullah, trans. *The Holy Qur-an: Text, Translation, and Commentary*. 2 vols. Karachi: Sh. Muhammad Ashraf, 1934, 1937. Reissued in revised form as *The Holy Qur'an: English Translation of Meanings and Commentary*. Medina: King Fahd Holy Qur'an Print Complex, 1989.

Arberry, A. J., trans. *The Koran Interpreted*. 1955; Oxford University Press, 2008.

Hammad, Ahmad Zaki, trans. *The Gracious Quran: A Modern Phrased Interpretation in English*. Chicago: Lucent Interpretations, 2007.

Jones, Alan, trans. *The Qur'an*. Cambridge: Gibb Memorial Trust, 2007.

Reynolds, Gabriel, with Qur'an trans. Ali Quli Qarai. *The Qur'an and the Bible: Text and Commentary*. New Haven: Yale University Press, 2018.

Habib, M. A. R., and Bruce Lawrence, trans. *The Qur'an: A Verse Translation*. New York: Liveright, 2024.

Translations of Selections from the Qur'an

Ayoub, Mahmoud. *The Awesome News: Interpretation of Juz 'Amma, the Last Part of the Qur'an*. N.p.: World Islamic Call Society, 1997.

Cleary, Thomas. *The Essential Koran: The Heart of Islam. An Introductory Selection of Readings from the Qur'an*. San Francisco: HarperSanFrancisco, 1993.

Cragg, Kenneth. *Readings in the Qur'an*. Brighton: Sussex Academic, 1999.

Kidwai, Abdur Raheem. *Daily Wisdom: Selections from the Holy Qur'an*. Leicester, UK: Kube, 2011.

Lings, Martin. *Holy Qur'an: Translations of Selected Verses*. Lexington, KY: Islamic Texts Society, 2007.

Sells, Michael. *Approaching the Qur'an: The Early Revelations*. 2nd ed. Ashland, VT: White Cloud, 2007.

The Qur'an in the United States

Birk, Sandow. *The American Qur'an.* New York: Liveright, 2016.

Einboden, Jeffrey. *The Islamic Lineage of American Literary Culture: Muslim Sources from the Revolution to the Reconstruction.* Oxford: Oxford University Press, 2016.

Grewal, Zareena. *Islam Is a Foreign Country: American Muslims and the Global Crisis of Authority.* New York: New York University Press, 2014.

Spellberg, Denise. *Thomas Jefferson's Qur'an: Islam and the Founders.* New York: Alfred A. Knopf, 2013.

Yuskaev, Timur. *Speaking Qur'an: An American Scripture.* Columbia: University of South Carolina Press, 2017.

Scholarly Companions to and Reference Works on the Qur'an

Archer, George, Maria M. Dakake, and Daniel A. Madigan, eds. *The Routledge Companion to the Qur'an.* London: Routledge, 2022.

Badawi, E. M., and M. Abdel Haleem. *Arabic-English Dictionary of Qur'anic Usage.* Leiden: Brill, 2008.

Iqbal, Muzaffar, gen. ed. *Integrated Encyclopedia of the Qur'an.* Toronto: Center for Islamic Sciences, 2013–.

Kassis, Hanna E. *A Concordance of the Qur'an.* Berkeley: University of California Press, 1983.

McAuliffe, Jane Dammen, ed. *The Cambridge Companion to the Qur'an.* Cambridge: Cambridge University Press, 2006.

———, gen. ed. *Encyclopedia of the Qur'an.* 6 volumes. Leiden: Brill, 2001–6.

Pink, Johanna, gen. ed. *Encyclopedia of the Qur'an Online.* brill.com/display/db/eqo.

Rippin, Andrew, and Jawid Mojaddedi, eds. *The Wiley Blackwell Companion to the Qur'an.* 2nd ed. London: John Wiley and Sons, 2017.

Shah, Mustafa, and Muhammad Abdel Haleem, eds. *The Oxford Handbook of Qur'anic Studies*. Oxford: Oxford University Press, 2020.

Sirry, Mun'im. *The Qur'an with Cross-References*. Berlin: De Gruyter, 2022.

Tottoli, Roberto. *The Qur'an: A Guidebook*. Trans. Angela Pitassi. Berlin: De Gruyter, 2023.

Web-Based Qur'an Resources

Altafsir.com (altafsir.com): the largest online repository of classical Qur'an commentaries in Arabic, many with accompanying translations.

Corpus Coranicum (corpus.coranicum.de/en): a repository of high-resolution images of early Qur'an manuscripts, with accompanying transliteration.

Islam Awakened, Qur'an Translation Pages (www.islamawakened. com): a resource that allows the user to compare sixty English translations, verse by verse.

Quran.com (quran.com): the most reliable current online resource for the Qur'anic text. Users can also select translations in English and thirteen other languages.

Qur'an Tools (quran.tools.com): a resource that allows the user to search passages, view interlinear translations and transliterations, conduct word studies, and generate statistics.

The Quranic Arabic Corpus (corpus.quran.com): a resource that allows the user to locate and analyze the grammar, syntax, and morphology of every word in the Qur'an; it includes a useful dictionary and concordance.

ACKNOWLEDGMENTS

Many of the surahs in this collection are revisions or substantial re-workings of translations that appeared in volumes 4 (2002), 8 (2006), 9 (2007), 13 (2011), 17 (2015), and 23 (2021) of the *Journal of Qur'anic Studies* (*JQS*), published by Edinburgh University Press for the Center for Islamic Studies at SOAS University of London. I am extremely grateful to the general editor, Professor Muhammad Abdel Haleem, a distinguished scholar and translator of the Qur'an, for providing my translations with a home and an audience, and to the journal editors, Helen Blatherwick and Ni'ma Burney, for unfailingly providing me with superb feedback and for offering their friendship.

One of the pleasures of completing this volume is having the opportunity publicly to thank the many other individuals who have encouraged, inspired, emboldened, bolstered, and critiqued me along the way. I begin with my Qur'an teachers: my late mother and father, Zubaida Ebramjee and Mahmood Toorawa, from whom I heard my very first words of Qur'an; the late Maulvi M. H. Babu Sahib; the late Baba Noormohammad Quadri; Shaykh Abdullah Diop; the Reverend Gerhard Böwering, S.J.; and Ustad Anwar Atchia. My Arabic teachers—Roger Allen, Adel Allouche, Amin Bonnah, Nazih Daher, William Granara, Adnan Haydar, Abbas al-Tonsi, and the late George Makdisi—opened a wondrous world to me, a world which fellow wayfarers have made it a distinct pleasure to inhabit: Sherman Jackson, Christoph Melchert, Herb Wolfson, and the members of RRAALL—Kristen Brustad, Michael Cooperson, Jamal Elias, Joe Lowry, Nuha Khoury, Nasser Rabbat, Dwight Reynolds, Devin Stewart, and Eve Troutt Powell. Devin, Joe, Michael, and Sherman have been urging me to keep translating since my earliest attempts in the mid-1990s and have championed my work since. This has also been true of Bruce Lawrence, who has consistently provided canny feedback and warmly promoted my efforts, both privately and publicly, and true of Gabriel Reynolds, who has also generously disseminated my work to the global Qur'anic studies community. I have also benefited enormously from working with my dear friends and comrades Philip Kennedy, James Montgomery, and Chip Rossetti in building the Library of Arabic Literature: I hope our attempts to transform the way premodern Arabic is translated is also somewhat reflected here.

Others who have supported me over the years in my efforts to render Qur'anic surahs in English, some unknowingly, include Sh. Musa Admani, Ebad Ahmed, Suzanne Conklin Akbari, Kecia Ali, Omar Alí-de-Unzaga, Waleed al-Amri, Sean Anthony, Mehdi Azaiez, Erhanfadli Azrai, Francesca Badini, Omer Bajwa, Karen Bauer, Corey Berrios, Sandow Birk, Ross Brann, Julia Bray, Clarissa Burt, Paul Cobb, Billie Jean Collins, Ashraf Dockrat, Salwa El-Awa, Emran El-Badawi, Alba Fedeli, Elizabeth Fowden, Zeshan Gondol, Aqiil Gopee, Fr. Sidney Griffith, the late Daniel Hoffman, Ruba Kana'an, Abdul Raheem Kidwai, Marianna Klar, Todd Lawson, Kenneth McClane, Faadhil Moheed, Susannah Monta, Sahar Muradi, Shady Nasser, Martin Nguyen, Rhodri Orders, Bilal Orfali, Sarah Pearce, Johanna Pink, Usman Qadri, Marcia Lynx Qualey, Tahera Qutbuddin, Nicola Ramsay, the late Andrew Rippin, Leyla Rouhi, Elias Saba, Omid Safi, Walid Saleh, Yasmine Seale, Asma Seddiq Al Mutawaa, Michael Sells, Emily Selove, Badrul Aini Sha'ari, Petra Sijpesteijn, Peter Simon, Nicolai Sinai, Ian Stevens, Mohammad Talha, Lucie Taylor, Mohamad Saleem Toorawa, Shabbir Ahmad Toorawa, Roberto Tottoli, Iqbal Umarji, and Hamza Zafer.

At Yale, I have benefited from the friendship and support of colleagues across the university, notably in the Department of Near Eastern Languages and Civilizations, the Department of Religion, the Department of Comparative Literature, the Whitney Humanities Center, and the Faculty of Arts and Sciences Dean's Office. I am especially grateful to Marta Figlerowicz, Christina Kraus, Frank Griffel, Adina Hoffman, Sana Jamal, Martin Jean, Alice Kaplan, Christina Kraus, Kathryn Lofton, Abdul-Rehman Malik, John Mangan, Nadine Moeller, Ahmed Nur, Maru Pabón, M. Arturo Perez-Cabello, Ayesha Ramachandran, Pam Schirmeister, Kathryn Slanski, Joanna Szczubelek, Gary Tomlinson, Kevin van Bladel, and Christian Wiman. I am most grateful to the Translating the Sacred group—Peter Cole, Robyn Creswell, Maria Doerfler, Steven Fraade, Supriya Gandhi, Eric Greene, Jane Tylus, and Travis Zadeh—whose meetings and workshops helped me focus many of my thoughts.

My heartfelt thanks go to Joseph Lowry, Nora Schmid, and Devin Stewart, who have been spectacular, endlessly poring over countless iterations and indulging my every query and every quirk. I am profoundly grateful to the magnificent Peter Cole, to whom I turned for a poet's discernment and sensibility, who spent innumerable hours plumbing and sounding my words (including a memorable meeting in the garden of the Elizabethan Club): his close guidance, his every alchemical suggestion, his every instinct, has made so much of this book better.

I close by thanking my uncle Firoz Toorawa, who was the first person to put me on the path of Qur'an translation and to have faith in my ability to undertake such important work; Peter Cole, for the astute suggestion of taking the volume to Yale University Press; my wonderful editor Jennifer Banks, for her enthusiasm for and embrace of this volume; Dan Heaton, for copyediting with acumen and sensitivity; the entire team at the Press, including Eva Skewes, Abbie Storch, and especially production editor Mary Pasti and designer Mary Valencia, for creating a book beautiful to hold and behold; my wife Parvine and our daughters Maryam and Asiya Tanveer Jahaan, for lovingly helping me conceive of this book, for always providing judicious comments, and for making my life a joy every single day; and Cotomili, our very own Mu'izzah, for his heartwarming companionship.

I dedicate this volume to the memory of my parents, Zubeida and Mahmood, my in-laws, Chotane and Areff, the incomparable Fareenani, and Baba Sahib—*rahimahum allâh.*

INDEX OF TRANSLATED SURAHS, PASSAGES, AND VERSES

This is a list of the surahs, passages, and verses translated in this volume. A boldface number indicates that the surah is translated in its entirety. A prime mark (') after a verse number indicates that only part of that verse is translated.